Stuart, Great Work, 10/10 well done . . .

David Gower (Yes, that David Gower)

"Watching With My Heroes" is a wonderful read, which will res-
onate with many who have attempted, but ultimately failed to
make the top level   Sports Journalist Association Website

He retails these tales with wit as well as dropping in plenty of
gossip along the way.   *The Cricketer* Magazine

The best sports book I've read since Hard Yakka. . .

Engaging, funny and insightful

There's no way I'm buying his book. Absolutely no way.

I've read many "my stories" from far more well known sportsman, but this is by far the best and most enjoyable one I've read
for many years.

A very intelligent insight into the strange world of pro sport

His many anecdotes are revealing and funny in equal measure
often providing a unique insight into the unseen clash of professional and amateur sports and the politics within.

I didn't think he could read, let alone write

A wonderfully honest account of the highs and lows of cricket.

A quite brilliant book. Had me in stitches so many times.

Hilarity from start to finish, an unexpectedly enjoyable read.

So good I read it twice. I had no idea it would be this good.

Poignant and funny in equal measure. A real eye opener.

"I don't care how good this book is, I'm not buying anything by him."

A really amusing book. Excellent from start to finish.

Watching with my Heroes

Best Wishes

Stuart.

Watching with my Heroes

Stuart Simmonds

First published 2017 by New Generation Publishing.
This edition published 2018 by Stuhead Publishing
www.stuhead.co.uk

ISBN 9781999318253

1 3 5 7 9 8 6 4 2

A CIP catalogue record for this book is available from the British Library.

Typeset by Ellipsis, Glasgow
Printed and bound by Clays, Bungay

For Jacky, Hannah and Lucy,
without you I would be completely lost.

For my family and my friends,
who have always looked after me.

For Mick and David, for without your help
I never would have seen anything

CONTENTS

*Updated in 2019

CONTENTS

Foreword
BY DEREK PRINGLE

All cricketers have hard luck stories – tales of near misses and what-might-have-beens. Some can niggle away over a life time, the passing years scarcely dulling that pang of regret or that indignant voice in the head. We bowlers should, of course, man-up and get over them except that, for those of us who propel the ball at more than 75mph, as Stuart Simmonds has done, the aches and pains, and their legacy, serve as constant reminders that the bad can so often outweigh the good.

My own particular tale of woe is reasonably well known. England's one-day team, clad in sky blue, were considered to be the best at the 1992 World Cup in Australia. Yet, despite that, we failed to clinch the trophy after losing to Pakistan in the final at the MCG – the third time England had lost such an occasion and the last time they appeared in one. Those white Kookaburra balls swung in that tournament and after snaring Pakistan's openers in that final for not very many, I trapped Javed Miandad, one of the era's great batsmen, right in front of his stumps. Not once but twice, in the same over.

There was no question that both were stone dead, Javed admitted as much afterwards. Umpire Steve Bucknor, though, perhaps sensing a dud final had he sent him packing so early, barely flinched and Javed went on to make a half-century, his 129-run partnership with Imran Khan the defining one of the match. Speculation as to 'what might have been' for me had Javed been given - an England World Cup victory, man of the match, CBE, marriage to Liz Hurley etc . . . etc . . . has been a piss-take game mates of mine have played ever since or at least every time Sky replay those two lbw shouts. As for me, I try not to dwell on it.

For Stuart, hard luck seems to have followed him around, at least as a cricketer. A keen and good club bowler, with wander-lust, he has been desperate and, in his own mind, desperately unlucky, not to break through into professional cricket with his beloved Sussex. When fate does conspire for their paths to cross, Stuart humbles Test and county batsmen with his canny seamers only to find himself stuck playing club cricket for the love and the beer. He reveals, with a self-deprecating candour, both his travels and his travails, to places like Australia and South Africa, as he tries to persuade various top level coaches of his merits and occasionally his weaknesses too. Tales of an all-night bender with Brett Schulz, a tearaway fast bowler for South Africa as well as the self-styled pisspot of Port Elizabeth (and a wasted talent if ever there was), vie with the 'brown adrenaline' he required to face the pacey Schulz out in the middle. Then there is the time he sends Andy Flower packing for a duck at East Grinstead, Stuart's home club, only to discover that the Sussex coach, whom he had hoped to impress, had been scoffing biscuits in the pavilion and had missed his moment of triumph.

There is a famous story about how Imran Khan spotted a teen-age Wasim Akram in the Lahore nets and picked him for Pakistan's Test team a week later, so there are fine lines between players being noticed and being ignored. Mind you, I reckon Wasim must have gained some kind of reputation by then if not for cracking heads then at least breaking toes with that fearsome yorker of his.

Stuart is not alone among talented club cricketers in believing that he could hold his own among pros. In the amateur era prior to 1963, and indeed in its immediate aftermath, such thoughts would not have been too fanciful. When I joined Essex in 1978, we had several club players making up numbers in the 2nd XI, though they rarely outperformed those on the staff. Yet, once professionalism entered the game, as culture rather than concept, it became little more than wishful thinking that amateur club cricketers might suddenly thrive, mid-career, in county cricket.

It doesn't stop them believing, though, which is great and part of the motivation for many. After all, it is the condition of the club cricketer to dream that he could play pro cricket and only a kill-joy would try to disabuse them of it. But the gulf is bigger than many envisage or even experience when they play against pros pre-season or in the odd benefit match – something the cricketers of Oxfordshire discovered when they turned up for a NatWest Trophy match against Essex in 1985.

On a flat deck at Chelmsford, Essex made 307 for six and promptly bowled Oxfordshire out for 81. I took five for 12 with what pros would consider fast-medium seamers and, without sounding too dismissive of our opponent's, they couldn't lay a bat on me. We had a drink afterwards in the sponsor's tent, as you did back then, and to a man they all said: "You don't look that quick on the telly." They were minor county players and therefore, in theory, a notch above good club players. The gulf multiplies exponentially with every step up you take and this incline was beyond them. And yet, part of cricket's beauty is that players of all abilities can cream that boundary like David Gower, the man Stuart identifies as getting him hooked on cricket, or bowl a jaffa like Jimmy Anderson, at least once. It is doing it regularly, against players of equal or greater ability than you, when the pressure is on, and in conditions more benign than most club players are used to, that separates the best from the rest.

Stuart was good enough to travel with his cricket, which is always to be recommended. When I wasn't picked for England touring teams, which was often, I spent time abroad playing in South Africa and Australia. On each occasion I returned an improved cricketer, something Stuart also experienced after his stints in Melbourne and Port Elizabeth, including, at his own admission, a better line in sledging. The route into pro cricket is never easy and many things play their part and not just talent. It is easier if you start young, something Stuart regrets having spent his late teenage years kicking a football around with his mates. I was fortunate in many ways, from the sporting talent bestowed by my parents' genes to the coach I had at school, the exposure to first-class cricket at Cambridge, and to the county I played for, Essex. England was a more bittersweet experience, the occasional high point surrounded by a sea of lows. With Essex I won five Championships, three Sunday League titles, one NatWest Trophy, and came runners-up in three Benson and Hedges finals, so there was certainly some glory. There were sacrifices, though – a life on the road and a salary well below that of most contemporaries from university. But I have few regrets save from underachieving with the bat.

Stuart seems to have been more frustrated than me but that may be because he once dreamed of big things, hoping they were within reach, but failed to grasp them for the myriad of reasons he neatly expounds in this book. But he frets too much. In a spot of cursory research, I spoke to a veteran of the Sussex club cricket scene and he told me, unprompted, that Stuart was exactly the kind of player you'd always want in your side – a very good seamer who'd bowl all day and someone who knew where the boundary rope was – in other words a player who was competitive on the field and companionable off it. Such words may not equate to man-of-the-match baubles, caps or first-class wickets but, in my book if not this one, there is no higher praise.

Derek Pringle

Foreword

BY DAVID BOWDEN

This is a book written with charm and honesty by a young man who has always had a belief in his own abilities and who is justifiably proud of his many achievements as a cricketer, coach, teacher and, more recently, as a businessman.

Stuart Simmonds describes how life in sport is not fair sometimes, with fine lines between talent, good fortune and bad luck, but also how important it is to seek to reach the heights of achievement in whatever activity one pursues. Indeed, he longed to challenge himself against the best players, particularly international cricketers, and had much success in doing so, both in the UK and as an overseas player in Australia and South Africa. It was unfortunate that he was injury prone and, on a number of occasions, was not in the right place at the right time to reach his ultimate goal of becoming a regular County professional.

The author is clearly fiercely competitive, always with a great desire to secure success. However, he is the epitome of someone who respects the *Spirit of Cricket*, which is to strive hard to win, but always fairly and with respect for the opposition, the match officials and one's teammates. Its not surprising, therefore, that he was both popular and respected – in the changing room and on the field of play, wherever he played.

I am much older that Stuart and nowhere near as good a cricketer as him, but I did play for Preston Nomads CC in the top flight of Sussex League cricket for many years. During that time, I had the privilege of playing with or against some 30 Test stars and realised the huge difference between Club, County and International players. There are very many excellent, high achieving club cricketers, but they are only able to participate once or twice a week, relying on minimal or no net practice and little or no essential one-to one expert coaching. There is a desperate need to ensure there is a highly qualified, active coach at every Premier League club, even if this means the exclusion of an itinerant overseas player. It is only when gifted youngsters, like Stuart, are taken into a County environment that they are given the opportunity to play or practice every day during the season that they can begin to maximise their potential.

As a pace bowler with over 400 league wickets and a good number as an overseas player himself, Stuart has many scalps of first class or international players and it is against that level of sportsman that one can measure how good one is – or, in my case, lucky! I had the privilege, during the 1977 and 1978 Sussex League seasons, to play against two of the sport's greatest stars – Tony Greig (at Brighton & Hove CC) and Imran Khan (at Worthing CC). Unbelievably, I had some batting success in both matches and was in for sufficient time to realise at close quarters just how wonderfully skillful, focused and determined they were. Imran had arrived in Sussex straight from a Test series in the West Indies, in the fifth match of which he had taken 6/90 for Pakistan.

Throughout my innings, I found him to be totally uncompromising, not appearing to accept that he was no longer playing in the ultimate format of the game! I was extremely fortunate to have had that exciting (and terrifying) experience and even more lucky to have come out of it alive – no helmets in those days!

As a cricketer, Stuart would be happy for me to describe him as a talented maverick. As a coach and a teacher, which are his true forte, he is equally gifted, making lessons fun, but always ensuring that things are done properly, in a smart and orderly way. He is passionate about the benefits that sport can bring to young people and is sensitive and fervent in the way he describes this.

In composing and writing this entertaining book, particularly in his excellent *Ramblings* sections, Stuart has shown himself to be perceptive and insightful, with plenty of good old common sense.

What is particularly impressive is that he is a man who having suffered the disappointment of not achieving his initial high ambitions had the wit and intelligence to leave the past without bitterness or resentment and move on to the next stage of life.

And, move on he has – with typical positivity and enthusiasm. He is now an important member of the wider *Sussex Cricket Family* investing much time and energy in seeking better facilities for children to become cricketers in the Crawley area, close to where he was brought up.

He is also back playing – for the Sussex Over 50s – back to the banter of the changing room, but now with a predominance of bandages and strappings!

Stuart is in his favorite sporting environment and long may it last.

David Bowden
Past President, Sussex Cricket

Introduction

From what I can remember, there wasn't anything too remarkable about Saturday 27, August 2016. The country was still getting to grips with the realisation that Brexit was actually going to happen, A levels and GSCE results had come and gone and, for most people, the summer holidays were almost over, meaning that autumn and then Christmas weren't far away.

Crawley Down against Felbridge in the First Division of the West Sussex League isn't quite the pinnacle of sporting greatness, I'll admit, but it's the place I found myself that day and so it was the place where I had to drag what little cricketing talent I had left into trying to help my team to victory. At my age – nearing a milestone birthday but still in total denial – to say I was well past my sell-by date was a gross understatement. In fact, I was so far past my sell-by date that you could say it was probably criminal for someone who was once a fairly decent cricketer to still be trying to hang on in the hope that something worthwhile and meaningful might happen.

My name is Stuart Simmonds and, without realising it at the time, August 27, 2016 was the day I finally decided that I'd had enough of playing cricket, a rather strange game that for many years now has driven me, defined me, frustrated me beyond belief and, at times, controlled me. So who am I, after all? To be honest, although there were times when I might have believed otherwise, I'm nothing extra ordinary and probably never was. I didn't play for England, I barely played any county cricket, didn't ever have a super model girlfriend, and I've never been lucky enough to have any lucrative sponsorship deals, or regular spreads in OK or Hello magazine.

It turns out that very few actually hit those heights, so why on earth am I writing a book if I haven't ever been there? That's a good point, to be fair, and if you think this is going to be one of those books where I tell you what it's like getting the phone call from the chairman of selectors informing me of my long overdue Test call up or the thrills or driving in a fast car with a lingerie model or pop star next to me or other such perks that come with being an international sportsman, then you're going to be very disappointed. So disappointed that you'll probably be asking for your money back, although, let's not kid ourselves here, there is every possibility that you haven't actually paid to be able to read it, because who is ever really going to read my story?

You see, there are thousands upon thousands of people like me all over the world, people who were very talented at a particular thing, be it an actor, musician or a sportsman but, for whatever reason, be it talent, luck, desire, patience or persistence, things never worked out as they once thought it might, or dreamt it would. This is not intended to drop into the "I could have been a contender" category because, to be truthful, that was never really a possibility, but I will also be honest enough to admit that for a while I could seriously play this game and there are many score-books, which will confirm this.

In all honesty, the main reason I'm writing this is firstly for myself, and my family and friends to try and make some sense of what I've managed to do with a huge chunk of my life and also to have something to remember when I'm older, sitting in my rocking chair fighting off the onset of dementia, wondering why I have chronic pain in my knees as well as the two big scars where my original hips used to live. Although I'd be delighted to be proved wrong, I'm not expecting my literary efforts to end up on the shelves of WH Smith or Waterstones.

These are my recollections and thoughts of how being pretty good at bowling a hard, red ball at three tall sticks allowed me the chance to travel the world, meet and make some fantastic life long friends, as well as occasionally rubbing shoulders with the very best and some of the most famous people the game has ever produced.

It's also the story of how I seem to have avoided ever having to get what you would describe as a normal, sensible job.

I hope you enjoy reading it as much as I've enjoyed writing it.

Stuart Simmonds
November 2016

1

ALL ABOUT ME

I grew up in the leafy surroundings of Crawley Down, a village between Crawley and East Grinstead in West Sussex and, for most children, that was a pretty good place to spend your childhood. Including me.

My parents, Malcolm and Janet, already had three children before I came along so they no doubt decided that they'd better stop, either because they had reached perfection with yours truly or, more likely, wondered what on earth they'd just produced as, apparently, I was a bit of a whopper. Dad was a senior executive for the oil company Texaco, travelling and working in London every day and Mum was a teacher at the local primary school, job sharing three days a week. Although she was never interested in moving up the career ladder, she would have made a brilliant head teacher. My brothers Paul and David and my sister Jane, along with a cat called Peggity, completed the picture and I remember, as I grew up, each of them leaving the family home, including Peggity who finally popped her catty clogs after an impressive innings of 19.

As a child I was probably quite easy to look after, once my efforts to escape my prison of a cot had come to an end. Like many children, I was happy to spend time in my own little imaginary world where I met Scott and Virgil Tracy and their Thunderbird machines as well as all the other characters from the Gerry Anderson programmes. Later, they were joined by a man named Bond. Thanks to them I had a fine old time and did not bother my mother – well not too much.

I got my sporting genes from my father who had been a good sportsman in his youth, playing club cricket and also representing Sussex at hockey. As neither of my brothers or sister were particularly interested in sport, my father was probably delighted that at least one of his offspring wanted to play with a ball in the garden although, at first, I was only really interested in football.

For a young boy, my early love of football was nothing unusual, and it was after getting a picture of Trevor Brooking that I became a big West Ham fan, something which I still am today. In fact, I and one of my daughters are current season ticket holders. I was a decent young player who scored goals for fun through the age groups and, for a while, I went to Ted Streeter's Brighton and Hove Albion regional sessions. Everything was going well until I was about 14 or 15 when it became obvious than neither I nor my team mates were going to be anywhere near good enough to make it through to the professional game. Sad but true; a harsh lesson in reality that I was honest enough to admit to myself.

As far as schooling went, my first port of call was Crawley Down Primary followed by Imberhorne Secondary. That changed when my father moved to Belgium with work and I pitched up at the British School of Brussels. It was the one place I really did enjoy, maybe because there was no uniform and no one actually knew me. Looking back, it seems strange now that, for someone who has spent so much time employed coaching sport in so many schools, I didn't actually enjoy my own schooldays. So much of it appeared to be nothing but a chore.

With all three educational establishments there seemed to be a common pattern. For me it was a combination of sheer laziness combined with my long visits to the world of the Tracy family and Mr Brooking -later followed by those giants of music, The Jam – that meant I didn't achieve what I could or should have done, much to the distress of my parents at report time. In short, I was a lazy bastard. Secondary school was by far the worst experience as teachers took little time to understand teenagers like me but I guess, with 350 other pupils to look after, they had little time to worry about a bored youth who just wanted to play sport and make people laugh.

When I look back on my time at school, those were the two things at which I excelled. I actually could make people laugh and I was pretty good at sport and so decided to concentrate on doing just that. When it was time for my careers chat with the hopeless Mr Morgan, a strange man whose head was miles bigger than it should have been, I was more than slightly worried when he told me he couldn't see any future career path for me in any shape or form. All he foresaw was some sort of factory work. He might have had a point, but that didn't stop me from thinking he was a complete bellend. My less than stellar stay at Imberhorne ended in 1984 when I gladly walked through its gates for the last time.

About 30 years later, while I was attending a dinner at the County Ground in Hove, one of my team mates asked me the slightly ridiculous question of whether I'd seen the Imberhorne Wikipedia page recently. To be honest, I didn't even know there was one and let's face why on earth should I? To my genuine surprise, in a list of famous alumni, there stood five names. The two

Fairbrass brothers from the band Right Said Fred, Nick Van Edde from Cutting Crew, who had the one worldwide hit "*Died in your Arms Tonight*" which probably still makes him a tidy sum in royalty payments, some random bloke who has a good job in a museum and, to my amazement, me; Stuart Simmonds, Cricketer. After the initial fits of laughter, I thought to myself that, with all those children going through the school every year, they surely should have produced some more famous ex pupils. Maybe it was the school that needed to try harder. Funnily enough, I never did get that letter from Mr Morgan congratulating me on making such a prestigious list. Perhaps he's still searching for me on some factory floor somewhere or other.

2

DAVID GOWER HAS
AN AWFUL LOT TO
ANSWER FOR

It's probably not fair to blame him too much, but I'm afraid David Gower really is the reason for my love of cricket. There were early efforts by my Dad to throw a ball around the garden and we did, as a family, play non-stop cricket but, for me, it was just a case of never being allowed to bowl, and then spending hours searching for tennis balls after my two older brothers had bashed them into the undergrowth. And when I did eventually have a go at batting – normally after Mum had intervened and said it was my turn – the bumbags would bowl far too fast for me and it would be back to searching for the ball all over again.

The summer holidays always seemed to be fondly remembered for long trips and hot days. Cameras would only come out when the weather was good which no doubt helped develop this illusion of constant sunshine and idyllic childhoods. Alas, the summer holidays could be quite tiresome if you had no one to play with and your sister or mother didn't want to go in goal.

The morning ritual of 1970s children's television would amuse me for a while with the Banana Splits and The Perils of Penelope Pitstop on the BBC constantly clashing with Stingray or other such gems on ITV. In the days before video recorders, what to watch was a decision that no young child should ever really be forced to make. Things, however, were about to change. I had, as usual, enjoyed my normal fix of morning television when coverage switched to cricket and, as I couldn't be arsed to move from the sofa, I watched the action unfold. It was England against Pakistan and, for a while, I saw a different game to the slightly less cultured version played by the Simmonds family. It quickly dawned on me that Mr Brearley and Mr Botham were rather better than my brothers although there were many times over the years I wished that Mike Brearley and especially Geoff Boycott would try the agricultural bottom handed slap. The bowlers could bowl overarm as well so that was also a cosmic leap for in my cricketing education.

Half an hour had gone when a certain D I Gower walked to the crease to face his first ball for England. My early amazement that he batted the wrong way around was soon forgotten as he effortlessly pivoted and, in a flash, the fielders were picking up the ball from the fence. At that precise moment, Scott, Virgil, James and Trevor were joined by David in my very exclusive heroes club.

With grace and style he made this new game easy to watch and, as a young boy, I was keen to go into the garden and copy him. Sadly, I still had to bat right handed but I tried to imitate everything else; the walk to the wicket, the way he twirled and picked up the bat right down to the way he casually stroked the ball. If I could have changed my birthdate and grown curly blond hair

I would have willingly done so, in order to look like my new idol. I was right in my element and spent the rest of that summer glued to the TV as my new friend David and his mates in white smashed Pakistan. It was also the first time that I understood why my Dad and Grandpa loved cricket so much. It probably helped that, as per usual, West Ham had been hopeless and had got themselves relegated. Cricket had started to provide a distraction from the fear of wondering whether Trevor Brooking was going to do the sensible thing and leave to play for a far better team.

Like most things in life that you love, there are the inevitable ups and downs, and with Mr Gower it was no different. He'd bat like a god one day, which would make me happy, then he'd be get out early for bugger all playing a shit shot and that would make me sad. To be fair to him, I'm sure he didn't do it on purpose but what he did that summer started me on a journey which would take me around the world, playing a game that I was determined to master in order to make myself at least slightly above average.

3

VILLAGE PEOPLE

It was time for me to see whether or not I had any natural talent for the game. Luckily for me my life was made easier by the fact that the local cricket club was no more than a couple of hundred yards away from home. I had been there a few times with Dad to watch and he had always told me that they looked a good side. For a young boy, the men looked enormous, appealed very loudly and seemed to hit the ball bloody hard. Surely they must be good enough to play for England, I thought.

The best news of all was that they had a junior section and so, in the summer of 1979, Mum made the important phone call to find out the evening's arrangements and I was set. My first coach/ manager was a lovely man called Colin Hunt, who is sadly not longer with us. He took me under his arm straight away, probably because his daughter was in my Mum's class at school and so didn't want to cause any upset by saying that her boy was hope-less and should stick to watching cricket on TV and dreaming that, one day, he'll be a Thunderbird.

Thankfully, after watching me bat and bowl on the first night of practice of the season, he told us both that I had lots of natural talent and if I listened and worked hard then I could be a good player. He also realised that I quite liked to be the centre of attention and encouraged me to do better each week. That was just what I wanted to hear and, from that moment, I lived for practice nights and any other time that I could get down to the ground and watch my new heroes. Unfortunately, there weren't many matches but that didn't stop me from soaking up every bit of advice and help I was given. With my friends in tow I would spend countless hours playing at the club in the summer. Given the chance, I would happily have lived there.

When I was finally asked to make my debut for the men's team in the first few weeks of 1983, there could not have been a prouder 16-year-old in the land. Obviously, the call came when someone had dropped out, opening the way for a promising youngster to come in and impress everyone by batting at No 11, fielding at third man all afternoon and having absolutely no chance of a bowl. That was the luxury that awaited me. All I had to do was get the go ahead from Dad.

Sadly for me 1983 was also the year for my O-levels and that meant revision. Well that's what it was supposed to mean. It's fair to say that my mind was not entirely focused on my studies at that stage of my youth, to the extent that I might as well have read a comic or drawn something pretty with crayons.

The thing about my Dad and cricket is that he was one huge walking and talking double standard. If I'd told him that I'd been picked to play football or been asked out on a date by a girl with enormous tits and dubious morals, then the answer would have been 100 per cent NO and I mean NO. For cricket however, there was always a very good chance and he allowed me to play on the condition I'd do plenty of revision beforehand. It was a kind offer

9

on his part but I'm sorry to say, I probably let him down, declining the chance to show him my morning's efforts in the shape of a quickly knocked up drawing of Thunderbird 1.

For a tall, spindly teenager, I probably wasn't expecting anything other than eating a huge plate of cricket tea, without actually contributing anything to the game. It was the annual President's XI match and so everyone seemed to know each other and they all greeted me with a warm call of "Hello boy". I wasn't too shocked when I was told I was batting at No 11 and so just waited for the jumbo portions of Mr Kipling's finest that would come my way. Again, I knew I had no chance of a bowl. In those days, you just played and played and waited your turn. For many young lads, their turn never did come along and so, unsurprisingly, they buggered off and did something else with their time. For the lucky ones, they sometimes got to go away with these strange new things called girlfriends.

The game was meandering along after Crawley Down scored far too many for about two wickets and then the President's XI replied with a hopeless effort meaning that it was time for the part time bowlers and buffet merchants to come on. When I saw the ball being tossed to Chris Wheeler, enough was enough. Chris, who I knew from watching similar games in the past, wasn't even guaranteed a bowl if he went into a Chinese restaurant. I walked over to the captain and asked if I could have a go. It was probably a similar situation to Oliver asking Mr Bumble for more gruel. Thankfully Chris thought it was a good idea, the captain agreed and I got my way.

The wicket keeper stood up to the stumps for the first time that afternoon as I marked my ridiculously long run up which resembled something from the West Indies pace quartet. I asked the keeper if he would like to stand back but surprisingly got no response. It's fair to say at this stage that, even as a youngster, when it came to bowling I had the ego the size of a small planet. I always had the ability not to give a shit about who was in front of me and how good they may or may not be. I was simply there to get them out and if they got in the way then that wasn't my fault either. It was an ability – or a curse – that never went away.

The radar didn't always work straightaway in the early days but it switched on pretty quickly for a 16-year-old. The first delivery was a bit of a loosener but by ball three the keeper had moved back as had the slip cordon. Ball four was parried by the batsman in front of his eyes and it looped up to be caught in the gully. I was up and running in men's cricket. The next batsman appeared to be shitting himself and so I let him have it for good measure. Caught slip in the next over. Chris Wheeler indeed.

I liked Neil Rhodes, next man in for the President's XI. He played for the second XI and was friendly with most of the players at the club. It's also fair to say that he was no Don Bradman and when my next delivery missed his nose by a few centimetres he asked whether I was looking to kill someone. Considering I was only 16, he probably didn't expect me to tell him that, next time, he was allowed to use his bat. They all must have thought: 'Who the hell does this kid think he is?' At the end of the over, the captain, Ian Pugh told me he was worried I was going to permanently harm his mate so I'd better come off. The fun was over for me, but the lasting impression had done me the power of good.

There were two people standing in the slips that afternoon whose eyes lit up the first time the ball hit the wicket keeper's gloves. David Stripp had been on the staff at Sussex in his youth and simply oozed class with both bat and ball. Even in his later years he had ability that others could only dream of possessing. Mick Mason was a fine opening bowler who had played in the higher leagues and was known for his supreme accuracy and very skilful he was too. He used to bowl about one bad ball a summer and had forearms the size of hams. He was also known for his loathing of anyone in front of him with pads and gloves on. From that moment, Dave and Mick saw I had plenty of potential and ambition and took me under their wings. They also loved the fact that, for someone so young, I had an unbelievable hatred of all batsmen.

These were the two people who, in the following few years, would do more for me than everyone else put together. I owe them everything. Without their patience, help, advice, guidance and encouragement, I never would have got anywhere. They are, to this day, my cricketing father and big brother rolled into one and I will never forget all they did to help me. In all the places in the world where I was lucky enough to end up playing, and with all the brilliant people I would go on to meet during my travels, no one came close to teaching me as much as those two.

4

START AND STOP AND START AGAIN

The next few seasons were a mixture of growing pains, experimenting and learning to live with the forks in the road that inevitably pop up every now and then. Generally, I was still in the 'promising' bracket, thoroughly enjoying spending six months a year with my new cricket family. The side rarely changed. We continued to hammer most of the opposition we came across and I was making steady and regular contributions. Such was the strength in depth of our team that most sides were beaten the moment we turned up and they saw who was playing. I provided some runs but, most importantly, I'd added what most sides couldn't offer – a young kid who could bowl quickly and, as I'm tall, the ability to make the ball bounce off a length. I also bowled straight and full when required, a surprisingly under-valued skill when you're playing against people with the batting ability of Kermit the Frog

The rivalry in village cricket in those days was quite intense with plenty of local bitchiness and old scores to settle. Most local teams were strong and could play to a decent standard, while still realising they were miles away from being good enough to play in the top flight of clubs in the Sussex or Surrey leagues. I'm all right but I know my level sort of thing.

To be honest, I was spoilt rotten. The wives would mother me to the extent that they would make me peanut butter sandwiches at tea as well as asking me countless questions about my love life and why a nice boy like me didn't show much sign of having a girlfriend. I was having a fantastic time – batting in the top five, fielding in the gully and bowling plenty of overs. But I also always had one eye on what might lie ahead. On the few occasions that we played at a bigger club, I would imagine what it would be like to play there every week, with the facilities and the prestige that went with it, and I was keen to try it out and see if I was good enough not to embarrass myself.

Within our side, and most likely in nearly all sides of a lower level, there was a built-in resentment towards the big town clubs. It's based largely on jealously as well as the fact that the larger sides often looked down their noses at the villages and were never shy of letting them know that they played at a pretty low level. Crawley Down were no different in that respect as, for all their dominance in the surrounding area, they needed to remember that it was still only village cricket. If we beat a bigger side on a Sunday, they would say that they didn't have their full side out and that, actually, they didn't try too hard on Sunday and that league cricket on a Saturday was what it was all about. Trouble is the resentment sticks and gets passed from generation to genera-tion meaning that lots of talented players were persuaded against trying their luck at a higher level on hatred and loathing alone.

It even got to the stage that there were there were two camps within our own dressing room. After I'd had a fantastic game against East Grinstead one Sunday, scoring 90 and then taking six wickets, I was told by Dave Stripp that it was time for me to move on to new challenges and that the club were holding my development back and not doing me any favours by continuing to pick me. Mick Mason, on the other hand, saw it differently. He told me the bigger clubs would piss me around, I'd hate it and be back in a season as had happened to a couple of players before me. Why go when you can continue to run in and scare the shit out of half of the players on our circuit, he said. The bigger league clubs were also not going to provide the peanut butter sandwich option either. Surely that had to be factored into the decision, I thought. Finally, the club told me that they wouldn't be picking me for the first Saturday fixture of the following season. Decision made then.

The general feeling from the dressing room was that they didn't want me to go to East Grinstead. Most of the players simply thought they were arseholes – no more, no less. Three Bridges was an option but I eventually settled on a move to Horsham CC for the 1986 season. They were arguably the biggest and most successful club in the south east, complete with a fabulous ground, their own county week every summer and a host of top class players. It seemed a good place to try my luck. My mate Nigel from college lived near the ground and was playing in their second team and I, being arrogant , thought I was miles better than he was, so surely I'd be greeted with open arms. As it turned out, nothing could be further from the truth.

Trying to break into the clique of talented, successful and grizzled first teamers proved virtually impossible and the second team was just full of grumpy bastards, all miserable and jealous because they couldn't get into the first team either. Obviously it had nothing to do with me. It became blindingly obvious that they didn't give a monkeys about where I came from and I'd better understand quickly that they weren't interested in my batting prowess, only my bowling, which thankfully they did rate. Any chance of fielding in the slips or gully were about as likely as me pulling a playboy model which, I'm afraid to say, were a big fat zero.

Although I'd passed my driving test by then, I didn't have a car so to get to my new club took me two bus rides and a train journey followed by a long walk to the ground. All that effort to be told I was batting at No 10. Oh joy. The teas were distinctly average as well. To be fair, there were some really good blokes playing there and they have remained friends to this day but it was clear that, with a top class overseas player and players brought in from Sussex on a regular basis, the chances of me breaking through were remote and I knew it. Strangely, they didn't seem too heartbroken when I left at the end of the season. In truth, I'm not sure they even noticed.

It was back to the drawing board and I came to the conclusion that I'd do better by going to a club that might be weaker but where I would be able to get into the first team which would allow me the chance to shine against the likes of Horsham, Eastbourne and Hastings. Perfect planning indeed. All I had to do was work out who were local enough and shitty enough for me to get a game. A minefield of a wicket would also come in handy. Only one answer then. East Grinstead here I come!

5

FUN IN THE SUN
AT WEST STREET

The early signs at my new surroundings were positive. It was a young side with some people I knew from school matches and a smaller core of older players who tried to keep us in check. The social side was better and it was closer to home so, all in all, things were looking up as we started the season. There was only one slight problem – we weren't the best. If I'm being honest, there were only a couple of players who would have got into another club's first team and the majority of us were second team standard. Sadly, we had quite a few who weren't even that good.

The old ground at West Street was a picture on a summer's day but the wicket was quite spicy and the old pavilion needed more than a lick of paint. The bare facts were that Grinstead were a side which hovered around the depths of the league year in, year out with nearly all the other sides seeing our annual clashes as a chance for an early finish and then back down the motorway with maximum points. Only Bognor appeared to be in a worse position.

The overseas player was a lad called Paul Cook, a talented all-rounder from Victoria in Australia. He was living with an older club member which he found a bit boring but he was an excellent bloke and gave me my first taste of what it must be like to play in another country, something that was starting to appeal as I came towards the end of my education. Tales of grade cricket and the Aussie way of life were made even more interesting as he was from Melbourne, which basically meant we had someone from *Neighbours* in our own dressing room.

I believe that, as a side, we hadn't had a league victory for three seasons so it was always going to be a tough year. My role was more as a batter and my bowling seemed to be rather under-used. I was easily the quickest at the club but the captain seemed to bowl a succession of military medium pacers including himself for over after over as I grew more and more frustrated under my new East Grinstead cap.

After the obligatory hammering on the opening day at Three Bridges the decision to try my luck at Grinstead looked like a poor one. The legendary Sussex League run machine Andy Meads pulled my first two deliveries over the pavilion and then, as I over-corrected, smashed the next two through the covers. Welcome to the league indeed. That was the difference. If I had bowled the same four balls at Crawley Down I'd have probably had four dots. Still, I was there to learn. I improved and ended up taking three wickets and was thrilled when Andy came up to me at the end of the game with a drink for a chat. He was very complimentary, which delighted me, as I'd watched him destroy many many attacks as a child and, secretly, he was a bit of a hero of mine. He was now my friend as well which was a bonus.

A minor miracle was to occur at Bexhill the following week,

when we actually won, chasing a decent score against a good side. They had a Kiwi who would go on to play Test and ODI cricket and we smashed him everywhere, myself included. The dressing room afterwards was awesome and to see the happiness on the faces of the older players who were so used to regularly getting battered was worth the long trip down to the coast.

As the season progressed, we were clearly improving, giving strong sides a run for their money and enjoying not being the whipping boys anymore. The return to Horsham went well for me as we came away with a strong draw and I got a few wickets and made a decent contribution with the bat. Some of their players didn't even realise I had stopped playing for them when I turned up with my kit. Playing for Horsham was Graham Roope, the former Test cricketer who had a long career with Surrey and had retired from the county circuit the previous year. He didn't strike me as the warmest human being and came with the pre-requisite ex pro's arrogance and disdain of anyone who hadn't played at the level he had. He wasn't shy of telling you, either.

Now I used to try to bowl this ball where I copied Mike Proctor's big whirling arms and bowled off the wrong foot in an attempt to confuse the batsman. I probably got someone out with it once and carried on using it thinking it was all part of a cunning plan from a master tactician. Actually it was utter bollocks and generally a waste of time. So why I chose to bowl it to the ex-Test player, I'm still not too sure. I came out badly, looked dreadful and Mr Roope smashed it bloody hard through the covers where only a flying Dave Tribe pulled off a great stop to save me from further embarrassment.

Now I'm not afraid to say that I have occasionally been called a c bomb but never so loudly and it had never happened at such a pretty ground. The nice man told me that I couldn't bowl that shit at him. I thought that was good of him. I thought long and hard about what to say and here was the chance to come up with a classic comeback one liner. I walked up to him, looked him in the eye and told him nothing better what he could do and where he could put his test caps. Hopeless. Not surprisingly it never seems to get a mention in the great sledges of our time.

Two balls later, I got one to bounce and the lovely Mr Ex Pro nicked it to the keeper, giving me my first first class cricketer wicket. I probably wished him well as he walked off. In every league there is the conversation between players of who would make it into the Wankers XI, a mythical side made up of the biggest tossers playing in your league. He'd might have made the final cut, if we're being honest.

We slightly flattered to deceive over the next couple of seasons as players came and went. I had my ups and downs and it can't have been easy to captain a side that contained so many young lads who could be a tad on the immature and frustrating side. And that certainly included me, I'm afraid.

6

RAMSEY STREET
HERE I COME

Some of the major decisions in my life seemed to come around after I'd received a bollocking from someone for some reason. This time I got two in the space of about three days.

I'd lost my way somewhat after college had finished and, forced by a huge overdraft, for some unknown reason I'd ended up working for a local company which sold taps and bathroom fittings. That's right, taps. People used to phone me up and order taps. Some with different coloured handles. All my hopes of doing something interesting with my life had appeared to vanish in the four walls of a soulless sales room. I hated every single minute of every single day I worked there and prayed that something interesting would happen to get me out of there. It never did. Libby the good-looking receptionist seemed to provide the only decent distraction from my daily chore of talking about washers, mixers and onyx coloured tap handles.

To make matters worse, the longed-for weekends were not so productive, partly on account of my worsening eyesight, and then I managed to catch glandular fever, which totally knocked me out. I could be a lazy little goat at times, but this was dreadful. The only blessing was that I escaped the office for a month and got a good sun tan while watching the Ashes. Sadly, it was the start of the Australian domination over England that was to last for years. The season was a write off and I only really managed to play a couple of games towards the back end of August.

The bollockings? First, Paul Cook laid into me, telling me to stop wasting my time playing football and concentrate on being a bloody good cricketer. He really did get stuck into me, even using some very rude words to get his point across. After telling my mates what an ordeal I'd suffered at the hands of the Australian overseas player, they then decided to do exactly the same. They all probably had a point. The outcome was that I quit my job, despite all its obvious perks and the open highway to the very top of UK commerce, and agreed to go and play a season in Melbourne at Paul's club.

I saved hard with the intention of playing the 1990/1991 Australian season. I managed to have enough cash to go travelling with a couple of mates, first to America and then on to New Zealand, which was a blast. We had made our way to South Island when we embarked on a trip called the Kiwi Experience, which seemed to be a must for all backpackers on the well trodden path around the southern hemisphere.

In a bar one night, I happened to catch the eye of a lovely girl from London called Jacky Morrissey who was on the tour herself. Well, you can guess the rest. We were both on our way to Australia and so travelled together around New Zealand and then saw each other all over Australia until we headed back to the UK through Asia. I obviously made a good impression on her when I walked into a crowed hostel and turned over to the cricket while they were all watching *Home and Away*. She should have known what she had to look forward to over the coming years. Thankfully I seemed to make her laugh and as she's bound to read this at some stage I'd better put on record that getting on that bus is probably the best decision of my life.

Sydney was the first port of call, hugely impressive and everything that it was made out to be. We stayed with a friend in trendy Potts Point which was a stone's throw from the famous Kings Cross area, where all the students and travellers stayed. It was also well known as the haunt for the prostitutes and call girls who plied their trade outside the bars and hotels. We certainly saw some gruesome sights and even if you'd been down to your last five-dollar bill, surely there would have been something better to spend it on?

Sydney to Melbourne on a coach might be the cheapest way to get there, but it'll take you over half a day to reach the place known as the home of Australian sport. I immediately feel in love with the place and felt right at home. Staying in Richmond, it was a five-minute walk to the MCG, the iconic home of the Boxing Day Test match which I was due to attend. The side I was planning to play for had engaged a full time pro from Lancashire and so I hooked up with a team called North Balwyn and did extra training with the grade side St Kilda. The standard was impressive, the work ethic and commitment way ahead of the UK. A register was taken at net nights and there were personal coaches who worked with small groups of players as well as proper fitness work to finish the sessions. No one slacked off or went home early and you had to have a bloody good excuse if you couldn't attend or you'd be dropped. Compare that with back home where six people would turn up if you were lucky. It was just a different world and I loved every minute of it.

I was desperate to impress and also aware that the Australian way of life was to trash English cricket in all its forms. It didn't help that Graham Gooch's tourists were receiving a hammering in the Test series, with the natives only really having time for Gooch himself and David Gower. All the others wouldn't have got into the Victoria side, probably only just about play grade cricket.

The whole club ethos was emphasised when, after the matches, everyone stayed around and went back to the club where, one by one, the team captain would stand up on a table and tell everybody about how they had fared that day and who had performed well. Right through from forth team to first. Then it was time for drinking which they were also good at. When it rained, everyone went down to the TAB, the local bookies, and it wasn't unfair to say that they didn't mind a flutter on just about anything that moved.

They took me to their hearts, liked the fact that I gave as good as I got and asked, on several occasions, if I was actually Australian. Everyone looked out for me, knew I was pretty skint but still kept asking me out. The whole club were in attendance at horse racing's Melbourne Cup which is Australia's equivalent of the Grand National. Pitched by the trackside, the drinking and gambling goes on well into the early hours. I barely won anything on the horses, but was so slaughtered that I probably wouldn't have known if I had.

Everything about the cricket was ultra competitive; the sledging was incessant as they hurled abuse at you from all angles the moment you walked to the crease. There was a bit of chatting in the Sussex League but nothing compared with this. Nearly all of it was pretty unsubtle and after a couple of games it just passed over your head. I did well, taking wickets regularly and even made my first decent level hundred so I look back at my time with much pleasure and a fair amount of pride.

One huge advantage for club players in Australia, and also South Africa, is that you have a month off towards Christmas and don't start again until the middle of January. This gives the players the chance to heal any niggling injuries and most importantly to look after their wives and girlfriends which in the UK could be distinctly hard at times. It gave me the chance to follow the Ashes and see some of the country. The MCG was definitely a bucket list moment and luckily for me David Gower scored a fine century at Melbourne and in true hero style, followed it up with an even better one at Sydney the following week. On the third morning he tore into Terry Alderman and Carl Rackermann smashing them to all parts of the SCG. I bloody loved that man and, after that knock, my full man crush was zooming into overdrive. Still when he got out last ball before lunch at the picturesque Adelaide Oval, playing an awful stroke, I couldn't help but agree with most of the English support when a word that rhymed with banker was used. I was so upset I could barely eat, but that I guess is what our heroes sometimes put us through.

Returning to Melbourne for the second half of the season, the absolute highlight was when we produced what is called an outright win. The format was that the matches were played over two Saturdays, with one side batting all day on the first one, then the other team seeing if they could beat it the next. It meant that players could build an innings and if the weather didn't intervene then it normally worked out well. What it meant though was that players put a huge price on their wicket, knowing that they might not bat again for a month. If you were an opener and batted late on day one, then you didn't want to get out otherwise you had to turn up the next week to watch and maybe have a little bit of time fielding late on, but it wasn't what you really wanted.

We produced North Balwyn's first outright victory over two weekends in late January/early February when we bowled out the opposition twice in one day to get a huge points haul and set off the biggest night at a club I could ever remember. If you had a dollar for every time the word "sensational" was used, you'd have ended up a wealthy man. The guitars even came out, with a song called *Khe Sanh* by the band Cold Chisel being sung on average every ten minutes. Its probably their equivalent of everyone in the UK singing *Wonderwall*. I'd actually never heard of Cold Chisel, but to be fair none of them had probably ever heard of The Jam.

The side were made up mainly of lads my age in their early twenties as well as a couple of slightly older ones who had kids and, for them, it was becoming a struggle. They all seemed to have mullet haircuts and drive old station wagons not seen since Jim Robinson had graced Ramsey Street with his presence. There was one man in his forties called Norman Hillier, with his big Aussie moustache and a fully paid up VB-induced pot belly. He was hopeless in the field but had been one of the best grade cricketers to have ever graced the Melbourne club scene. We batted together many times and you could see he was simply a class act the way he wore bowlers down then ripped the attack apart when he was set. He was the only player who was sledge proof from the opposition. I just rested on my bat handle at the other end and admired a bloke playing a different game from the rest of us. He refused to give up, stating many times that you're a long time retired and you won't be able to play when you're dead, so bollocks to everything else and just play as much as you can. I thought he had a fair point but, for some strange reason, Norman was on his fourth marriage when I met him.

We drew too many games to make the hallowed top four places in the league that meant your season continued for another month as you played the semi finals and then the final of the competition. In our last match, I witnessed our young aborigine spinner suddenly leave the pitch and go walk about. He literally just walked off and keep going. Did it at least once a season apparently, so when it happened the club looked after his kit until he turned up again.

Like most countries in the early 1990s, Australia was suffering from a major recession and that made finding casual work pretty hard which, in turn, meant I was running through my savings to the point that it was nearly time to phone home and ask to draw on some of Grandma's money. It wasn't much but it helped. Cash reserves were running so low that I told the club I might have to go home early, but I was having a good season and they managed to find me some coaching work in the afternoon at the local schools and then at the indoor cricket centre which was owned by the captain and his brother. I thoroughly enjoyed it, seemed to make the kids laugh and fancied doing a badge when I returned to the UK so, without realising it at the time, I'd made the first strides into what would be a new profession. I think if I'd been bang average then they'd have just told me to start travelling home and not come back.

7

I SUPPOSE I'D BETTER
GET A JOB THEN

After the season was over, Jacky and I travelled up the east coast to the Great Barrier Reef then across to Ayers Rock and down towards Adelaide, finally flying to Bali from Perth. The ludicrously long coach journeys gave us plenty of time to discuss what on earth I was going to do when I returned to the UK. The sad realisation was that my travels and pseudo cricketing career were coming to an end, rather too quickly for my liking. It was time to grow up and face certain realities. Although I hung onto the belief that Thunderbirds still might be real, there was no hiding from the fact that it was time to go and get a proper job.

The general idea was that I had to find a career I actually enjoyed otherwise I'd be as good as useless to anyone stupid enough to employ me. I certainly wasn't rushing back to sell taps in a hurry. Something sports related seemed to be the order of the day, something I was generally interested in so my low boredom level wouldn't be tested too much. Sadly, Jacky put her foot down when I suggested that a career in the porn industry may be the way forward.

Before any of this could happen, I had to make my way across Asia which was made harder after I got Bali belly so badly that I was wiped out for a month and lost so much weight that I looked like I'd been on hunger strike. I knew the sweet and sour looked like a plate of bubbling shit but I didn't expect to get what was coming to me. A couple of hours later I'd lost half my body weight and was lying on the bathroom floor of a £1.00 a night room, talking to a rat that had come up through the middle of a drain. I was so delirious that I might as well have been chatting to Roland Rat. Not really what you want to see. Even worse, my tan had faded – I was whiter than when I left home.

Returning to England was a relief though my Mum freaked that I'd lost so much weight and she spent the next two months trying to feed me up to look like my previous self. The strange thing about being away is that it's only when you return that you realise you've actually missed nothing. Someone's split up or got together, maybe someone's been fired or got a better job but, in reality, everything in your world is pretty much the same as you left it. Thinking you were missing out on so many things when you were away was probably a waste of time. People want to know you are back safely and had a good time, after that they're not too bothered.

Britain had not been recession-proof either and trying to get ahead on the work front was proving harder than expected. With Jacky's help, I sent an excellent letter and CV to all the major sports manufacturers and retailers and waited to see what Postman Pat would bring me in the way of job offers. It was easy to add up as the total amount was zero. Just polite rejection letters.

A brief spell trying to flog hospitality packages at the major sporting events seemed a good idea until I was handed copies of Yellow Pages and told to start at the beginning of book one and work through to the end of book six, and then do it again. That idea fell instantly into the "f@@k that for a laugh" bracket and was swiftly discarded. There must be something else. . .

I had signed up for a place on my coaching award course, which took place over two weekends at Great Walstead School in Haywards Heath. Run through Sussex County Cricket Club, it was my first real taste of anything to do with the county and the presentations and drills put on by the national coach Les Lenham and his son Neil were superb. I had come across Neil before for, as a youngster, he had been in the prodigy bracket, breaking all sorts of schoolboy batting records. His rise to the top appeared to have been halted by the fact that he seemed to have poppadums for fingers and every time Allan Donald or Malcolm Marshall hit them they snapped in half. Not even specially made protective gloves could keep him on the park long enough for his talent to shine. But he was a bloody good coach and he entertained us all during the breaks with his tales from the county circuit. It seemed like a pretty good life for the ones lucky enough to hang around long enough to have a career.

The upside of all this was that Sussex were launching a new coaching scheme designed to go into schools and get more children playing the game. Thankfully I did well on my exam, got an excellent grade and, even better, a job offer from Sussex as one of the coaches on the shiny new Seeboard scheme. The hourly rates of pay plus the travelling expenses were excellent and I could fit it with helping my mate Bob on the building site, which improved my fitness and cash flow. The banter was pretty good too. Within a month, I'd gone from politely being told what I could do with my hospitality package by a man in the Yellow Pages to being paid well to play cricket with kids. Quietly, I thanked the Lord for his good grace and tried not to look back, for both I and the big man upstairs knew that getting paid to play non-stop cricket was not really classified as proper work.

8

LOOKING IN FROM THE OUTSIDE

The thing about doing a coaching badge is that it bears zero similarity to what it will actually be like when you instruct a group of school children. In an exam situation, you will be provided with a group of well behaved, attentive youths all helping you show the examiners you can run a session properly while getting all your coaching points across. You foolishly think that all children will be like this when you arrive on the doors of a school, resplendent in your brand new Sussex tracksuit, looking to all concerned like a proper cricketer. They'd do better to tell half the group to piss around and not pay the slightest bit of notice to your words of wisdom.

It's not an understatement to say that my first attempt at being a new all singing, all dancing supercoach didn't quite go according to the script. Thankfully having a mother who was a teacher was a big help and she gave me a crash course in group management.

Take absolutely no nonsense, threaten to send them to the head-teacher and remember boys, I'm the comedian around here, not you – that sort of thing.

I was paired for certain schools with an old coach by the name of Pat Cale who had worked at the county for many years running the Sussex Young Cricketers, effectively their pathway to the professional game. A club player by trade, he had helped many, many players on the way through to the first team dressing room but when I met him it was towards the end of his career and he had been pushed aside for younger, more energetic coaches. He had a lovely manner with the children and it seemed he picked his favourite schools to match his favourite pubs throughout Sussex.

We were at a school in Eastbourne one afternoon doing basic bowling. Pat asked me to do the demonstration which was a bit of a risk as he'd never seen me bowl before. Thankfully it was a day when the ball came out nicely. "Where have you been hiding?" he asked. He suggested a trade-off. He would organise for me to go to the County Ground in Hove for a sort of trial if I agreed to attend a seminar for some sort of pyramid selling scheme that he had got himself into. I accepted instantly with the full knowledge that I was buying nothing. The only problem was that I didn't quite know how to get to Hove.

I'd only ever been to the ground at Hove once before. I was taken by a friend's father to see Sussex play Leicestershire one Bank Holiday Monday on the understanding that it was the chance to see David Gower in real life rather than on the telly. I needn't have bothered as he was out lbw second ball. Still the constant stream of ice creams made up for the rather enormous anti climax that had just occurred. All I remember was lots of deckchairs and lots of old people who clapped politely when someone did something of note.

For someone who liked cricket, I had to be honest and admit I knew nothing about the county I was supposed to support. I knew Imran Khan the brilliant Pakistan captain played there and that they had some brothers called Wells but that was only because they went to school with my cousin in Newhaven. There were a couple of young pros from my coaching course, including Jacob Dean, a left arm spinner and good bloke. Apart from that they could have been anybody walking past in the street.

I had no idea that cricketers were paid for only six months of the year and I had no idea they received so little. It's nice to get paid to play sport but some were on peanuts, many still supported by the bank of Mum and Dad while they chased their dream and, in many cases, chased their parents' dreams. Lots of them had second jobs like postmen, some ran their own small businesses while others went overseas to play, coach and get a suntan.

The two people who Sussex employed on a winter coaching contract met me at the old Arthur Gilligan stand where the indoor nets were housed. My first impression was that the ground hadn't been painted since my last visit in 1980. The nets were freezing cold and looked pretty threadbare but both Keith Greenfield, a batsman who captained the second team, and Peter Moores, the regular first team wicket keeper seemed friendly and took a genuine interest in me. They must have seen hundreds of prospective players each winter all hoping to get a game for the county but it didn't show, which was kind.

Time to bowl then. Peter Moores fancied a net so strapped his pads on and Keith Greenfield talked me through what he was looking for if I was hoping to play at a higher level. I remembered Moores smashing a rapid 80 playing for Eastbourne a few years earlier when he was particularly savage on Trevor Francis, an old schoolmate of mine. He would go on to find fame in later years by becoming England's Head Coach, not once but twice. Thankfully the net went well, I managed to impress and was asked to come and play for Brighton and Hove where Keith was playing. He could monitor my progress and, if I did well, there was a chance that I could get a game in the Sussex Second XI. I just wanted to see how good I was against what I considered proper players.

When it was all over, I had some time to kill so walked around the ground and eventually ended up outside the players' dressing room and walked into the members' bar where the outgoing captain, Paul Parker was sitting. He had been a bit of a childhood hero of sorts for me and despite only ever playing one test match, he was a top-drawer batsman and possibly best known for being an absolutely outstanding fielder ranking alongside David Gower and Derek Randall as the finest of his generation. He was also an extremely bright man, sitting there quietly reading a book that was so thick it made War and Peace look like something from the children's Ladybird series. He asked what I'd been doing in Hove and so I told him that I'd just had a trial and he wished me well. When I asked him about the enormous book he was reading, he said it was all about Virgil. "He's one of my heroes," I replied, to which Mr Parker looked genuinely impressed. However, what came next might have shattered that initial illusion. "I love Thunderbirds. Does that book have the story about when they landed the plane on the remote-controlled cars? That's one of my favourite ever episodes."

He looked at my rather strangely, and said something shocking about Virgil actually being a philosopher and not a puppet. That was news to me. Probably not a great first impression if I'm being honest, but he was off to Durham pretty soon so I prayed it wouldn't come back to haunt me.

Bizarrely, I had now entered the brand new world of a million players around the globe trying to "make it". To some you sound delusional, dropping names barely anyone has ever heard of, while others look at you as if to say you have got about as much chance of breaking into the Bank of England as you have of breaking into a professional sports team. The one rather large problem I had – I was 25 at the time – was that you were supposed to be doing this kind of thing at a much younger age than I was trying to do it at. It was a large problem that would never really go away.

9

I HOPE THEY PAY
PETROL MONEY

Any day you get a cheque, is a good day I suppose. But the day you get your first cheque for doing what I was doing is an excellent day. To be honest I felt like a smug little bastard when I presented it to the nice young lady behind the counter at the Nationwide Building Society. There was even a little Sussex CCC crest on the cheque as well for good measure. However, like most jobs you do, no matter what you do in life, you need those cheques to keep coming in on a regular basis and it soon became clear that, as with the cricket season, cricket work was a seasonal thing.

The move to my new club of Brighton and Hove hadn't really worked out. They'd relocated to a new ground opposite the greyhound stadium and the politest way of describing it was that it wasn't Lord's. After playing a couple of pre-season inter club matches and doing reasonably well, it didn't feel like a good move and the thought of running up the very steep hill trying to impress the right people seemed a non-starter. Another minus was that the person who had got me there, Keith Greenfield, had started the season in the Sussex first team so wasn't playing either.

I had an escape route because Lewes were keen for me to join them. I had done my coaching badge with many of their players and must have impressed. In terms of match winning ability, they were a better bet and the ground had the huge advantage of at least being flat. They also had a trump card in the shape of an Australian overseas player by the name of John Boyd, a proper opening batter who spent the year commuting between the Sydney first grade scene and the Sussex League. He was keen on me joining Lewes to open the bowling and he even persuaded Keith Greenfield to let me move from his beloved Brighton and Hove. If I did well, the right people will know about it, he always used to tell me. For him, ambition was not a dirty word and he liked the fact that I was desperate to better myself.

Lewes had a proper team, full of experienced league players and youngsters all of whom had been on the books of Sussex at one stage. All except me, to be honest. They had won the league a couple of time in the previous few years and, back then, were usually one of the top five teams in the county. Luckily, I started well and picked up wickets regularly so, all in all, it was proving to be an excellent move. The fact that I had moved to a big side near the coast changed people's perceptions even though Lewes were in the same league as East Grinstead. The miles were clocking up fast as I made at least four trips to Lewes each week plus all the coaching work that was coming my way as I became more familiar in the Sussex set up. Thankfully the petrol money came in handy.

Trying to gauge the standard that was required to play at the next level wasn't always easy. As a general rule the Sussex first team players were engaged with league clubs but rarely played and that certainly applied to the established capped ones. That meant it was only the better first class overseas players and the young professionals who appeared every weekend who you could compare yourselves against. One such player was a young Ed Giddins who turned out for Eastbourne. Although Lewes won our match easily, and both Giddins and I took four wickets, that was where the similarity ended. He put in a performance that highlighted the different levels between certain players. He had pace and control as well as the best seam presentation I'd come across at that stage. He was simply a class act at an age where he would only get better. A huge maverick as a bloke, he didn't appear to take anything too seriously and so looked as if he played without any pressure. By the end of the season he had broken into the Sussex first team and, despite some well documented forks in the road, was playing for England a few years later. In all the seasons I played in the leagues I never saw a better home grown player. He ended up becoming a bit of a star in the world of poker once his cricket career had finished – something which doesn't surprise me one little bit.

The influence of John Boyd and the other senior players was rubbing off and I finished the 1992 season on a high when I was picked to play against Sussex II's for the League XI in the last game of their season. Leaving it as late as I had in terms of trying to cling onto any chance of getting onto the professional staff, it was finally the chance to impress that I'd been waiting for and I was genuinely excited about being selected. Like a young child playing their first matches, I watched the weather forecast at every given opportunity for around a week leading up to the match and as I drove down the A23 to Hove, the first signs of the forecasted rains started to hit my windscreen getting heavier as I drove into the ground. So you can imagine my huge disappointment as I watched in horror as the heavens finally opened and the match was abandoned without a ball being bowled. Over the years it was normally injury that turned to kick me in the nuts at the worst possible moments, this time I'd been chewed up and spat out by the weather gods. As anti-climaxes go it was like being told you can go to bed with one the Corrs and then finding out that it's actually going to be with the brother.

What it did show me, though, was a glimpse into the lives of the people who played at that level. It appeared that there were several different types of people sharing the dressing room for several different reasons. The capped player captaining the side who was wondering whether he'd come to the end of the road as younger players had overtaken him into the first team and there were the fringe players who were hoping and longing for another chance to prove they could cut it at first team level, but deep down knowing that the winter would either see them released or moved further down the pecking order with a winter signing or two from another county. There were also the players who had realised that it just wasn't going to work out financially, especially if they had mates earning much higher salaries in the world of commerce and they were simply sick of being skint. Be it an excuse or a dose of hard reality they knew that the axe from the committee members would be only a matter of days away, meaning that a P45 and a message of good luck for the future was all they had waiting for them.

On the other hand, there were the very young players who still had all their hopes and dreams intact. Their long-awaited contracts would surely come in the next year or two and they would be up and running on the first steps of the ladder that they hoped would lead to Test cricket.

September for me meant that my chance to impress had vanished for another six months and I wondered whether it would ever re-appear after the Sussex coaches wrote an article in which they said they saw no real sense in playing any players over 21 or 22 years of age from the leagues. That article was duly filed in the "Oh Bollocks" category.

10

BUT I'VE NEVER MET
IAN BOTHAM

Getting car insurance can be a pain in the arse at the best of times and my efforts at speaking to the nice young man at Norwich Union somewhat stalled when the subject of what I actually did for a job came up. To be fair, it was hard enough to explain what I did to my friends so to the insurance man it really wasn't making much sense. There was no box to tick that said cricket coach, let alone sports coach, and that was proving a hurdle for our man at the other end of the phone, despite his exemplary telephone manner. At that stage I was driving a fairly average car, probably not worth more than a couple of grand, so I wasn't expecting my insurance to be more than about £200. Problem is he still can't bracket me. Finally, the quote came out – at £3,940! After picking myself up from the floor and asking him in my best BBC voice whether he was trying to be a comedian, he then uttered the phrase that has always stayed with me.

"But what if you're driving with Ian Botham in the car and you have a crash?" He had a point, just not a very good one.

Trying to explain the difference between someone who coaches at schools and clubs around Sussex and someone who plays in the England Test team with a national treasure like Mr Botham should have been simple until the man from Norwich Union informed me that the only option his computer was offering him was "professional cricketer" and that involved the possibility of driving to matches with someone potentially very difficult to insure. The chances of Ian Botham sitting alongside me in my Montego were about as likely as driving around town with Elvis Presley in the back and both of us signing *Viva Las Vegas*.

Thankfully my sarcasm won the day and, eventually, he put down "teacher" on the form. With my Ian Botham no claims discount the premium went down to £185. I told him that if I ever did have the great man in the passenger seat, I'd send him the balance.

Trying to find your level as a sportsman can be rather tricky at times, especially when you drop down to play with your friends on a Sunday. Like many players, I was moving between top level club stuff on a Saturday and then playing with my mates back at Crawley Down on a Sunday. It was here that I received the biggest swing in my fortune to date and it wasn't a particularly pleasant one from my point of view. On the Saturday, I played against Chichester, a superb club side and arguably as strong as any I played against in the UK. They regularly reached the last stages of the national knockout cup and had won the Sussex League for the previous three seasons.

On an early day in May at the Stanley Turner Ground in Lewes, I bowled a decent opening spell, removing Jamie Hall, the Sussex opener, Allan Elgar, the overseas player who opened for Western Province in South Africa, and then Jon North, another contracted

Sussex pro. Well done me I thought as I received plenty of pats on the back walking off from a job well done. I'm getting quite good at this, I thought as I drove home that night. Tomorrow was the village knockout match between Crawley Down and fierce local rivals Colemans Hatch. What could go possibly go wrong? As I found out, the answer to that question was plenty.

It all started fairly well as I bowled my first five overs for the miserly amount of one run with a wicket to boot. The big cloud on the horizon was a cricketer called Gary Mason, a talented lad who never fancied trying his luck at a higher level. In truth, I thought he was a better bowler who could also hit a very long ball as he had an extremely good eye but he only seemed to come off a few times a season. This Sunday was going to be one of those days. After only conceding one run in my first five overs, the last four went for 68 runs as, whatever I threw down, he returned in spades. There were some truly enormous blows as the ball flew out of the ground several times per over. My final figures of 9-4-69-2 were horrific in the pre T20 era. And, to finally top it off, during the run chase, I was our last real hope when Mr Mason returned to dismiss me first ball with an unplayable swinging yorker that would have got me out every single time. At times like that, it's just best to shake hands and then go home and crawl into bed, which is exactly what I did. To be honest, it took me several weeks to get over it. In all the years I played, and against all the fantastic players I had and would go on to play against, I never ever got a hiding anything like the one I received that day. For the Colemans Hatch players, it was probably their greatest day ever. For me, it was by far my worst and I vowed it would never, ever happen again.

By the end of the 1993 season, I was at something of a crossroads. In truth, I knew I hadn't had the best of seasons. Any real chance of making a late charge into the Sussex set-up had been extinguished by an elbow injury that meant I was taking pain killers as if they were Skittles, and a-not-disastrous-but-less-than-normal wickets return meant no one was noticing me anyway. I was playing for a mediocre Lewes side coming to the end of their time as a really good team. I was also, in all honesty, financially up against it, which didn't help as I was engaged and we had a wedding to pay for. Time to do something different, I thought.

I had been approached by a few mates and a couple of committee members to return to East Grinstead for the following season. With a massive new pavilion and sports hall being built from the proceeds of the sale of the old ground at West Street, the prospect of getting lots of extra coaching work was hard to ignore. It also helped that, by then, Jacky and I were living near the ground so there would not be so much travelling and the social side looked promising too. It was even possible that Jacky could meet some people on a Saturday night who might not want to discuss cricket or football! And we could finally use the dining room table to have a proper dinner party.

Before the ink was dry on the transfer though, a call from Sussex police caused a bit of a panic. I was asked to go to the station to discuss my payments from Lewes Priory CC which, in my dire financial state, was news to me. The story behind Lewes' fall from grace could be traced back to the appointment of a rather bizarre man who went by the name of Stuart Hutchinson Blue. He had seemed to have done the decent thing and agreed to become the club's treasurer which, as anyone will tell you, is a pretty thankless task. The trouble was, though, he was actually using the club's money to pay his rent in Brighton and, when the club realised what was going on, it was well and truly in the mire to the tune of a few thousand pounds. It transpired that he had one meeting with the police when he claimed several players were getting paid far more petrol money than was the case, including some who didn't even have a car. By the time he was due to return to answer more questions, he'd done a runner faster than you could say "The Talented Mr Ripley". He even had the same spectacles and BBC accent as him. His back story of being orphaned was found to be, like everything else, utter bollocks. If he'd told you he was wearing two black shoes, you would have done well to look down and check.

The tragedy was that the two blokes who introduced him to the club, Jon Roycroft and Mike Abington, were as decent and honest as anyone you could meet. They obviously felt guilty by association and, over the next few years, they chased and tracked him down all over the globe, finding women conned out of inheritances and money stolen from so many different people that it would have been funny if so many people hadn't been scammed. Sadly for Lewes, they never really recovered and it serves as a harsh lesson to all clubs to beware of accepting the first person that offers to do a job that no one else really fancies. Even worse, the club then went on to fall out of the county leagues and into the realms of East Sussex cricket.

For me and the others accused, the police decided that they'd heard enough new evidence regarding Mr Hutchinson Blue to not ask us any further questions. Come to think of it, I'm not actually sure whether that was his real name of not and, to be honest, I wouldn't believe him even if he said it was.

11

I AM ACTUALLY IN
EASTBOURNE ON
A THURSDAY

As anybody who has had the pleasure of planning their own big day will tell you, weddings can be the biggest test of anyone's diplomacy skills, especially when parents and relatives start getting involved. It is also an unbelievably expensive day, especially when the cost of stag and hen nights and the obligatory honeymoon to foreign shores gets added onto the bill.

Now I'm sure many new couples and parents will testify to the fact that modern weddings are more horrifically pricey than in 1994; this was after all a time when mobile phones and the internet didn't exist and so we never had to go through the twitter delights of a jackystuart photoshoot online and the countless pages of wedding planning and other details on www.pleasebuymeabloodygreatpresent.com.

What it was, however, was gruesomely expensive when you're earning peanuts pretending to yourself that cricket might somehow turn out to be a worthwhile and sensible career choice. In order to try and bridge the gap between paying for the big day and going out onto the street with a begging bowl, we reluctantly decided that although we were both working full time, we could ease our financial issues by earning an extra two hundred pounds a months leading up to the wedding. That's a hundred pounds each by my calculations. Jacky thought that despite travelling up to London every day, she would try and find some work behind the bar of a local pub or something similar for her contribution whilst I stumbled hopelessly around for a few ideas to keep my end of the bargain.

What I wasn't expecting was for the future Mrs Simmonds to suggest one evening that I become a sperm donor. She had seen an advertisement in one of the many magazines that she'd read on the train home, pointing to the possibility of well paid work in the above field. After some research, we found that the nearest clinic was in Eastbourne and that the reserves down on the south coast weren't in great shape. Surely a match made in heaven awaited.

Better still was the fact that Sussex CCC had given me three schools and an evening session at a local leisure centre in Eastbourne on a Thursday and so that would tie in nicely from all parties' points of view. With the added bonus of a cash payment of £50.00 per deposit made, I would be able to double my monthly contribution to the Simmonds wedding fund.

Once the forms had been filled in and returned, it was all falling into place quite nicely. Surely the idea of hundreds and thousands of little versions of me running around the country would be a fantastic proposition for the United Kingdom, especially as I was going to be getting paid handsomely to take part in one of my all time favourite pastimes. Added to the fact that I got money to play cricket with children all day this really did seem too good to be true. If there was somehow a way for me to be paid to watch Thunderbirds then that surely would have completed the holy trinity of me being possibly the spawniest bastard of all time.

We were all set for a month's trial and so the Thursday activity would consist of :

9.45am	Leave home in East Grinstead
10.00am	Arrive in Eastbourne
11.00am	Coach at St Andrew's Prep School
12.15pm	Lunch
12.45pm	Coach at Parkland Junior School
2.20pm	Arrive at the Clinic
2.30pm	Smash one out
2.45pm	Leave Clinic with £50.00 cash
3.15pm	Coach at Willingdon Primary School
4.45pm	Coach at Sports Centre
6.30pm	Depart from Eastbourne
7.30pm	Arrive back home in East Grinstead richer than when I left at 9.45am

All was running smoothly until some annoying Doctor decided to throw an almighty great spanner at my plan of money making Nirvana. When I sat down with the pot-bellied man in his white coat, he informed me that the clinic was looking for donations of the highest quality. He even told me that in my language, my deposits needed to be in the test class bracket in order to have the best chance of success. It wasn't bad enough to be constantly reminded season after season that you might just be slightly lacking in the pace department to make it to the top table, but now I had to come to terms with the fact that my bullets might not be Premier League standard.

Three weeks later and obviously under huge strain at not knowing my fate, the kind doctor delivered the minor bombshell that my offerings were of a high grade, but not the rocket fuel that the clinic desired. Fathering children should not be a problem in any shape or form but my time of being paid handsomely to bash one out whilst still being able to fit it into my hectic coaching timetable was suddenly called to a halt. Heart breaking though it was, I'd still been paid £300 for doing something that wasn't the most arduous task I'd ever been asked to perform in the workplace. Probably the hardest part of the whole venture was managing to refrain from cracking any smutty and totally uncalled for jokes whilst at the clinic. They'd have heard them all before no doubt.

In all honesty, it probably took me at least twenty minutes to get over the rejection as I returned to normal Thursday activities from there on. However, for four glorious weeks in the spring of 1994, every time a clumsy defender was rude enough to call me a wanker playing football on a Saturday afternoon, I could happily look him in the eye, safe in the knowledge that at least I'd been well paid to be one as well.

12

DOES ANYBODY ACTUALLY WATCH THIS STUFF?

According to statistics sent out by the ECB in 2015, just over two million people watch county cricket every season. This does include figures for T20 which has bumped the figures up somewhat since its inception in 2003 but, in truth, the amount of people going through the turnstiles around the country every year aren't that impressive. It's not only a problem in England, it's happening all over the cricketing world where people just have no real interest in watching first class cricket. Some follow it religiously and have done for many years, through newspapers and, way back in the day, on Teletext, and then onto Cricinfo and the internet. Today, we also have various means of social media to keep people in touch but, truth be told, barely anybody goes to a ground and watches a game live.

This means that, unless you are an avid follower of county cricket, you will have no idea who any of the players are or what they might actually look like. County cricket gives people the chance to meet and get to chat with their heroes, providing the access that other sports can't offer. For some, this is part of its great charm and appeal. However, in terms of recognition, it didn't much matter if you added the England players into the discussion as well. And if you needed any proof of this – although some of the egos around the circuit might have thought differently – then you just needed to go and coach in a local school.

Pick a school, anyone, anywhere in the county or the country for that matter and you'd have got the same answers. Pick two teams for a match and then quiz the captains. Can you name me the Sussex captain? No, it's not me, thanks. I wish it was, but it isn't. Honestly, it's not. Any ideas? None? OK, let's ask another one. Where do Sussex play their home matches? I'll give you a clue – it begins with the letter H. No, it's not West Hoathly, that's a small village near here, isn't it? Anybody else know? No, it's not London, and that starts with the letter L, doesn't it?

OK, can you name me the really famous cricket ground in London, then? It's really really famous, anybody. . . . . . and it went on and on to the point where you have no choice but to ask who lives in a pineapple under the sea and then listen while every single one of the kids screams SpongeBob Square Pants.

You could probably ask a question about football and nearly all of them would know the answer but, when it comes to county cricket, you haven't got much of a hope which is a shame. Even with the advent of YouTube and other multimedia influences, you would have thought that it might have made it easier but I'm not so sure.

To try and catch the imagination a few years back, the ECB came up with the idea of producing a sticker book for the school children hoping that it would have the same effect as those ever-popular football versions that dominate the playgrounds all year long. Our cars were full of books and sticker packets that we used to give out at every session and visit we did during the summer. To be fair, the children took to them and it did create some interest but, back then, Test cricket was still live on terrestrial TV which was a definite help. The players loved them too and would plaster pictures of themselves all over their lockers and cricket coffins. None of them would admit that their stickers were regularly swapped for something more valuable. I'll swap you 50 Justin Bates and 50 Toby Pierces for your shiny Mike Atherton sort of thing. From my point of view, it was quite frustrating to see someone you'd played against on Saturday scoring an unimpressive 18 and then only taking two for 55, getting his picture stuck into a child's sticker album come Monday. If I had a pound for every time someone asked me if I had my own sticker, I'd have had a hell of a lot more money than I was actually earning.

The move back to East Grinstead had proved a successful one and we had started the season well. Most of the older players of yesteryear had retired or moved to the seconds and we had the backbone of a pretty decent side. For this, we had stormed into the final of the Sussex League Cup, knocking out some prodigious opponents along the way, which meant a trip to Hove with your mates. For me, it would be the first of many times that I played in a decent match hampered by a bad injury. A painful shoulder prevented me bowling properly but I managed an economical spell as we romped to a seven-wicket victory over Brighton and Hove, with our Australian overseas player Adam Shipard taking the man of the match award with an excellent 70 not out. For Grinstead, it was the first time they had won any meaningful silverware and was a nice two fingers up to all the detractors around the county.

The onset of the mid twenties age slump had come up without me really noticing and, for the first time in a few seasons, I'd stopped worrying about trying to impress people from the county as I knew I had virtually no hope of getting signed. Getting kicked in the elbow playing football before the start of the 1993 season had really put one final nail in that coffin. What was there to do now, I thought. I still had the personal ambition to be as good as I could be and I felt I wasn't quite finished yet. I was only 26 and thought I had years left before it was slippers and pipe time.

Towards the end of that summer, a couple of significant events happened. First, I had briefly mentioned to Jacky that being the overseas players was a pretty good gig for the winter and, to my great surprise, she suggested I try to go back to Australia to play A grade. Go and see how good you, she said. Get it off your chest so you don't sit back in your rocking chair as the old git you're bound to become and wonder whether you were ever good enough – that sort of thing. We weren't even married then and here I was being offered a ticket to the other side of the world. Maybe after living with me for a couple of years, Jacky thought that six months without me and more importantly with no cricket would be a blessing. It was a stunning gesture none the less and, once you've made that kind of offer, you can't really take it back.

Then, one afternoon, she happened to be watching a programme about the 1994 South African's tour to the UK, the first since the end of apartheid. It included lots of information about the development programmes in the townships and that had sold it to her. Why not cast the net a bit wider and possibly include South Africa in your travels? She'd always wanted to go to Africa so it seemed a sensible option. There was clearly an advantage to her doing African Literature at University and I was beginning to look like the beneficiary.

Oh, and on September 17, two weeks after the end of the cricket season and just before the start of the football season, we finally got married at Crawley Down village church with all our friends and families in attendance. It was a quite brilliant day followed by a honeymoon in Thailand. When we returned, I thought I'd better start saving or, more importantly, get more work as although I probably didn't act like one, I was now a sensible married man.

13

DEAR MR BACHER

There's one thing about trying to save up for something – it assumes you have the necessary amount coming in at the other end to put the money aside instead of spending it. In a nutshell, that was the problem, as more important things appeared to take preference such as sofas and linen, kettles and garden furniture. I did have a full Sky TV package though, which in those days was viewed as a bit of a luxury.

In order to address the financial straits, we decided we would have Adam Shipard, our returning overseas player, and his South African girlfriend, as our lodgers for the English summer and their rent would go towards paying for the trip. Adam had spoken to his club in Perth about me going over as their pro for the 95/96 winter and they seemed keen. The problem was that I had used my working visa when I played in Melbourne and I had no chance of getting another one. Cash in hand work was out of the question for them and you never really knew whether you'd get past the Australian immigration. That was proving to be a fairly massive spanner in the works.

Not to be deterred, Mrs S decided to follow up on her South African idea and, out of the blue, wrote to Dr Ali Bacher at the United Cricket Board in Johannesburg asking about the possibility of me coming to play and coach in their new development programmes, as her desire to visit the Republic was almost as great as mine. Before too long his office had written back, giving all the numbers and addresses of the main unions around the country. It was time to start scribbling.

I'd been fortunate to meet a man called Chris Fletcher who was the newly installed youth development officer at the nearly brand new East Grinstead sports club. He gave me plenty of coaching work and I told him about my plans to go to South Africa. Fletch had been a cricketer himself with Sussex and was a fabulous coach, especially with the younger age groups. He had also spent many seasons playing and coaching around the Cape so his contacts book was brimming with extremely useful numbers. He went through the unions that weren't for me and told me to concentrate on either Border, Eastern Province or Western Province. Too much Afrikaans up in the other parts of the country, he said. You'll never understand anybody in six years let alone six months. As it happened, he was keen to get back there as well and was privately looking for coaching jobs himself. All he had to do was persuade his wife to go back and he would have been out there before you could say pretty mountain.

The fax machine as well as the typewriter went into overdrive as we contacted his mates and then waited for a response. We waited, and then waited some more.

We had to have a contingency plan if the letters didn't prove fruitful. We knew it was a long shot and that it might come to nothing. Quite simply I'd run into a wall in terms of where my coaching career was going. Former county players with 200 first class games under their belts were always going to beat me to a job even though perish the thought that some ex-players made dreadful coaches.

Two coaches I worked with that winter were Martin Speight, the sublimely talented young batsman, and Peter Moores, the keeper whose work and fitness ethic were second to none. Speighty started coaching East Grinstead in the winters and we became good friends. He appeared to be a bit of a maverick and I could see how he disagreed with some of the senior players at Hove. His approach to the game was very positive and this was reflected in his coaching style. He made me work hard on my batting skills in order to turn me into a genuine all rounder, spending hours on the very unpredictable bowling machine at Hove. My batting improved until one day he ramped up the machine a tad too much and the ball thudded into my private parts at a rate that turned my bollocks into matching ear rings for a few seconds. He thought it was hilarious until he realised that I wasn't getting up and he had to call an ambulance. I was off work for three days, which is awkward when you have to tell someone that you're not coming in because your gonads are currently the size of two fully inflated space hoppers. Try explaining that to the children.

As a coach, it was instantly obvious that Peter Moores was destined for greater things. His style, knowledge and enthusiasm were infectious and he was instantly the sort of bloke you wanted to impress. Youngsters and adults alike loved working with him and I learnt so much from him that winter. He understood club cricketers and didn't make the mistake of some of his colleagues of thinking that, unless you had played at the same level as them, you weren't entitled to an opinion. He realised there were many hundreds of club players who could do as good a job as many players on the current staff. After all, they got to play and practise every day while the others had to go to work and hold down a job. Moores had a few years left playing for Sussex but, once he retired and put on the tracksuit full time, he quickly rose to the top. To watch him work was worth the journey alone.

As the season was due to start we had the grand opening of the new multi million pound pavilion and sports hall at East Grinstead. It was to be a whole weekend affair with a huge gala ball on the Friday night followed by an invitational cricket match on the Saturday. It probably wasn't a great idea for half our team to get legless the night before, but it was a bloody good night none the less. The match promised to be something of a trickier affair. The committee had arranged for ex-Sussex captain Paul Parker, who had only just retired from Durham the previous September, to put together a side to play East Grinstead in a 35-over match. Former England captain Mike Gatting was the celebrity who, along with the mayor, cut the pretty blue ribbon on what was the coldest day in living memory. Also on hand were the entire Sussex playing and coaching staff that was en route to a pre-season camp in the West Country. So, all in all, there was a decent turnout to watch the upcoming proceedings.

In fairness, the Paul Parker XI were a really good side made up of some current and only just retired players. Parker himself, plus David Graveney, Simon Hughes, Vic Marks, Ian Smith and David Syd Lawrence were among the players turning out and, as if they weren't already strong enough, they had also called upon Zimbabwe's finest, Andy Flower, who had scored an unbeaten 150 against Pakistan the previous week. I think it's fair to say he was in good nick and form wasn't an issue.

As is usual with these games, the pros bat first and set you a total that they pretty well know you're not going to get, and that was not far off what happened. In front of all these people of note, it was important for me to at least get the first ball somewhere near the cut strip and not embarrass myself. The sight of the number two ranked Test batsman in the world at the other end does make the job a little harder. My fat arse it does! He can go and stick his Test caps up his arse for all I care. It's time for the ego to kick in and for me to get this bloke out, no more no less. And so that's what I did, much to the horror of the watching public and, more importantly, the organisers who had banked on the very talented Mr Flower destroying the clubbies.

The first ball nipped back and caught him on the crease right in front of the stumps. I went up with the slips, screaming to the high heavens. That's plumb lbw. Jesus Christ, surely not. . . Not out, to a relieved committee. Don't forget they are here to see him bat and not you bowl. He struggles with the next four deliveries as I attack the stumps. Last ball and I trap him in front again, this time giving the umpire absolutely no option but to raise the finger. A Flower, lbw Simmonds 0. In fairness to him I might have thought that I did him for sheer pace six balls in a row, but in all likelihood, it was so cold I think his arms had frozen solid and he couldn't actually get his bat down. Still, a good one to put in the bag, I thought. For me, there was more to come as I bowled a seven-over spell where the ball was doing everything. It was a rare, strange feeling knowing that you appeared to have the ball on the end of a string and it seems just a matter of time before the batsman duly obliges and nicks it to the keeper. As the next two pros went back in the same direction as Mr Flower, there was a strange feeling around the ground as if I was putting on a show that would surely impress the watching people from Sussex. My teammates were all saying that they had to notice me now – it was starring them in the face. Two edges through the slips were the only runs I conceded and I honestly could have had more than the three wickets I picked up. In one over, I beat Paul Parker's outside edge every single time. By the end of their innings, I taken three for eight in seven overs against Test and county opposition and those figures did me an absolute disservice. Now, I told myself, wait until you walk off and see if someone talks to you from the county. Fletch was beaming, as were quite a few others, but, in an exchange that possibly summed up my fate regarding my career, a Grinstead member went up to one of the Sussex coaches and asked whether he'd been impressed by what he'd just seen. He replied that he'd been eating his lunch from the over-stocked buffet and hadn't been watching. You wonder why you bother sometimes . . .

The second half of the match was about the potential re birth of David "Syd" Lawrence as a fast bowler. He famously smashed his knee to bits so badly playing in a Test match in New Zealand a few years earlier that he'd been forced to retire. However, he was attempting to make a comeback and used this game to see whether the joints would withstand the enormous shock he was about to put through his body. His run up was outrageous as he stormed through the crease sending the ball at a terrific rate through to the keeper. The openers Steve Pollard and Dave Tribe, didn't know what had hit them. The players watching from the balcony thought it was all very amusing until they realised they might have to have a go themselves. Pollard, one of the best openers the league has seen, tried to play the ball with his gloves up round his visor and then get down to the other end so he could watch and see if his partner would fare any better. Dave Tribe had a bit of that slightly mad opening batsman about him and loved it quick but, when he was so late trying to cut one that it went over the slips for six, I think even he was bricking it.

After Syd's five-over onslaught had finished, the game meandered into the mismatch it was always going to be, as we never really got close. In the bar afterwards they were extremely complimentary about my spell and I got a very nice bottle of champagne for my efforts as the man of the match. Andy Flower and Simon Hughes were a couple of terrific blokes and stayed chatting for hours afterwards but the Sussex team had long gone and so, in reality, had any last hopes.

What on earth was I going to do instead of cricket? That was a constant question going through my mind. Whatever I did, it still needed to sports related and, after a beer or six with my friend Dan Evans, I plumped for a slightly left field move into journalism. Dan had worked on the sports desks of both the Daily Mail and The Mail on Sunday and was always ridiculously generous with his time and advice. We went back years and, after talking to him, I signed up at the London School of Journalism and was all set for brand new start in September. I was excited and, to help me with my potential new career, I even starting reading the newspapers.

Meanwhile Jacky, who has never been known for her patience, decided she couldn't wait any longer to see if I was going to get any offers from South Africa so she phoned from her office in London and had a bit of a shock when she got through to the CEO of Eastern Province. She introduced herself to Mr David Emslie and explained why she was phoning. To her amazement, he was reading my CV as her call came through. Now if that wasn't fate then I'm not sure what is. The stumbling block was the airfare so when Jacky said we'd pay it; the deal was as good as done. She told Mr Emslie that I'd call him in ten minutes, which I did and, by the end of the day, I had a generous faxed offer of a job from the Eastern Province Cricket Board based in Port Elizabeth. I was running round like a dog with two dicks.

So my potential new career as a journo was put on hold as I prepared to get ready to up sticks and be an overseas professional.

Most people couldn't believe my wife was letting me go and some even thought we were somehow getting divorced. It spoke volumes about some people's marriages, I suppose. In all honesty, it was an unbelievably kind gesture from Jacky and I will never forget it. Ever.

14

ALONE AT THE ARRIVAL GATES

Time passed quickly as I prepared for my African adventure. The English summer finished in a damp squib as the last three matches were washed out and only the announcement of the touring English team for the first official tour of the Republic since the end of apartheid pushed football off the back pages. For me, it was a case of getting my affairs in order and leaving enough money in my account to pay my standing orders. An unexpected dental bill made a huge dent in that but if you don't visit the dentist for four years, then you shouldn't complain too much when you end up having more fillings than Jaws from the James Bond films . . . and a bill to match.

The plan was for Jacky to come out for a month at Christmas and then again in February so we wouldn't be apart for too long, but it would still be hard. We had talked about Jacky quitting her job and coming with me but she'd been progressing brilliantly at work and it would have been a waste to stop her progression. As departure day loomed, it seemed that we'd be apart for ever.

I knew the trip would be a huge chance for me to see if I was good enough to play at a higher level and my coaching skills would surely improve with the exposure to working with some different people and seeing alternative ways of doing things. From the advice I'd received from people who'd done it before, it was clear that I needed to be open minded and embrace my new surroundings otherwise I'd be eaten alive. I didn't want to be just another overseas English player that went home with their tail between their legs and their confidence shattered.

To say that saying goodbye at the Heathrow departure gate wasn't pleasant would be an understatement. I felt awful leaving Jacky behind and the thought of a flight to Port Elizabeth with more stops than a London bus didn't make it much easier. With stops in Amsterdam, Greece and Johannesburg, it was finally a relief to touch down in the Windy City of Port Elizabeth and I was looking forward to the welcoming committee that would surely be there to meet me.

In fact, there was a welcoming committee of none and I walked around PE airport double checking my correspondence to see that I'd actually come to the right place. Eventually I had to charm a girl from the car rental desk so I could phone the Eastern Province offices. Sounding slightly embarrassed on the phone, my new boss David Emslie said he was fully in charge of the situation and left for the short drive to the terminal. It was only when I arrived at the offices that his secretary told me he'd been expecting me the following day. He hid it well. I was immediately impressed by how welcoming everyone was but it's quite daunting meeting so many people in such a short space of time and trying to remember anyone's name was virtually impossible.

My job was based at St George's Park. The Test match venue

steeped in history and also the home of Port Elizabeth Cricket Club, the oldest in the country. With the new Duckpond Pavilion, it was hugely impressive and a far cry from the County Ground at Hove with its peeling paintwork and rusty metalwork. I was assigned to play for a club called Gelvandale in the northern areas of PE and work at a variety of places including St George's, and the schools and clubs in the city. Dave made sure that I was kitted out in shiny new sponsored clothing with an even more impressive sponsored car to boot. I really did look like Billy Big Balls.

My flat in central PE wasn't quite ready to move into so, for the first two weeks, I stayed with Dave and his family in Walmer and his wife Sandra looked after me. The last thing she probably needed was another cricketer landing on her doorstep but, if that was the case, she didn't show it.

When your new boss comes to you on your first night and tells you that you're going to his mate's bachelor party you don't really say no, even if you've been travelling for nearly 24 hours. It would have appeared rude anyway. A very enjoyable evening was had by all, including the legless groom-to-be. It became clear by around 2am that, in 1995, the drink driving rules were largely there to be ignored and you didn't even think about trying to get a taxi. So the thought of getting into the car with your new boss who appears to be in a far worse state than you are less than 12 hours after meeting him is a fairly precarious one. Thankfully, he managed to drive us both home and, over the next six months, we would get on famously. A top man indeed.

There appeared to be something of a family feeling for the people who worked at St George's Park and I was quickly included into that. Players, coaches and all sorts of strays and hangers on would walk through the offices almost at will, all interested in the new Englishmen who was working there. There was Nick, a tiny lad who lived across the road and reminded me of an Oompa Loompa who was definitely on the spectrum. He just walked in and helped himself to a drink from the fridge whenever he fancied while, occasionally, helping out with the ground staff. He was often accompanied by a girl in her early twenties who was never without her Bible, from which she quoted regularly. The other thing about her was that she was ridiculously easy on the eye and, from what I had heard, she was very friendly with several of the players. Funnily enough, she seemed to know quite a few of the international players as well when they came to play in the city. Must have been for Bible study, obviously. When I was introduced to her she asked me immediately whether I'd played first class cricket and when I replied that I hadn't she said it was a shame. Strangely, the women in the office were never that keen on her.

Club cricket was held in very high importance in the town and the A grade competition was extremely strong and just what I'd left the UK to have a go at. In those days, unless you played for South Africa, you would have another job to run alongside your cricket. Eastern Province was made up of farmers, estate agents, bankers and chemists and they all played for their clubs who paid them and expected them to play properly. So each weekend you could easily end up playing against six or seven first class players added to the best clubbies and overseas players that the region had to offer. Two or three sides I played against that winter would have easily been stronger than most county sides. The best thing was that they did not care about how the younger players in the EP under 19 side had done, they couldn't give a toss about that. It was your performances week in and week out in the leagues that counted and if you were the player in form and there was a slot in the EP side, you got it. Warren Jamieson took loads of wickets for Union CC and when there was a place going for an opening bowler, he was the player who was put on the plane to

Cape Town to play against Western Province – he got Dessie Haynes out in the first over to boot. I couldn't wait to get started.

With this in mind, I watched in trepidation at the PECC nets as a sharp left armer performed his arts and extremely useful he looked to. He would have walked into any side in the Sussex League. When I asked who he was I was told he played in their second team and was nowhere near getting promoted. If that was the case, maybe I thought I should bolt out now, make up a designer injury and try to save face before I got completely found out as the imposter that I might sadly turn out to be. It did cross my mind to quietly hide myself away for six months and hope that nobody noticed I was missing.

15

ARE YOU SURE YOU'VE GOT THE RIGHT BLOKE?

After a couple of days, I finally got to meet my new team mates at a hastily arranged pre-season fixture against Union CC. Sadly there was no chance of play as, even in South Africa, it can hose down and ruin the best laid plans. Still it gave me the chance to get to know my team mates before the season started for real in a couple of weeks. There seemed to be some whispering going on about their new overseas player and his credentials – or lack of them – added to the fact that he's also a white bloke.

It's always nice to be wanted by your new team but when two players greet you with an autograph book, you need to start worrying and, for that matter, so should they. The problem arose because of my name and how it is spelt. How it is not spelt is Symonds, as in Andrew Symonds who, at that stage, was deciding whether he was English or Australian. He'd been playing for

Gloucester in the English summer and had broken the long-standing record for the number of sixes hit during the season and so was hot property. With a bit of glorified Chinese whispers, the lads at Gelvandale thought he was coming to play for them that season. I decided to sign the autographs anyway and made it look like I did this sort of thing all the time. If it made them feel any better, I'd hit at least four sixes the previous season so they had nothing to worry about. I have a feeling that the fee for Mr Symonds to come and play might have been slightly higher than the actual fee for Mr Simmonds.

As a side, Gelvandale were the mavericks of the league, capable of brilliance one minute and utter stupidity the next, and it was my job to try and bring some order and sanity into the side. There was no lack of talent but the mental attitude of the players was way behind others of the same age and that would eventually hamper their progress when it came to higher honours. What they didn't have was much bowling and so they were glad to see that I could actually land it in the vicinity of the stumps on a regular basis. They loved me and took to me instantly because I was there to help them and that's all they really wanted. In return it was very easy to love them back.

I was thrilled to be asked to play in a pre-season match between all the EP squad players and a few of the English pros out there for the winter and saw it as an immediate chance to impress and get an idea of what the standards would be like in the following weeks. Kepler Wessels was the current captain of the EP team and had been in charge for years. For many people, he ran the side and everything at the club with an iron fist in that no-nonsense Afrikaans manner where just by looking at you he gave you the impression that it'd be a fairly good idea if you did what he said. Apart from playing Test cricket for two countries plus World Series Cricket and county cricket, as well as captaining his country at the last World Cup, he didn't really have much going for him to be honest. Although he'd only just retired for international cricket, he was clearly still the best batsman in South Africa and everyone knew it. He was also a fitness freak and a martial arts expert to the extent that he's probably the hardest bloke I've ever met. Forget the probably – just don't piss him off, I told myself.

With this reputation in mind, umpires were so scared of him that you would have to blast all three stumps out of the ground before any of them would be brave enough to raise their finger and send him on his way. The players knew it as well but, sadly for me, I hadn't twigged.

It had all started so promisingly. My first two overs were on the money and Kepler played me with surprising respect. The trouble started with the first ball of my third over. It bounced a bit more and he nicked the cover of the ball through to the keeper who took it in front of first slip. What a result, I thought. I'll be dining out on this one for years. It was so out there was actually no need to put your finger up, Mr Umpire. So why isn't he walking off?

When the umpire then said not out, I somewhat lost the plot. I had a little support from the fielders but they'd seen it all before and weren't that surprised. The real fun started when Mr Wessels informed me that I might want to go back to my mark and bowl another one. I can't remember my exact words but they went along the lines of I didn't care who he was or how many Test matches he'd played, that was just plain old cheating. If I'm honest I might have sworn, at least a couple of times. Amazingly, he didn't look best pleased with me offering my opinion. When he offered his thoughts on the subject, I responded in my best BBC accent by calling him some very rude words before taking the advice of some of the fielders who tried to impress on me that any minute now he was likely to remove my head from its shoulders, just to teach me a lesson on why you don't talk back to someone with so many black belts.

The game drifted on, Kepler, moved onto his obligatory century but I never gave in and didn't stop trying and finally had him caught at gully in the last couple of overs. The real fun started after the match when I was summoned by an extremely stern looking David Emslie to explain myself. He looked furious. Good one Stu, you've been sacked after less than ten days in the country, a new low even for you. It couldn't have been further from the truth. He told me that Kepler had been impressed with my attitude and commitment and the fact that I wouldn't back down. Stunned and hugely relieved, I then found out that he wanted Dave to put a net bowling squad together for him to practise in the mornings. For this, Dave bumped up my monthly money to which I didn't object and I accepted quickly. I shook his hand and buggered off before he could change his mind.

So the moral of this story, children, is that when they talk about the spirit of cricket being all-important, you can tell them it's all a load of old bollocks really. All you need to do is shout your mouth off at a national icon and in return you'll get yourself a pay rise. It's as simple at that.

16

RUBBING SHOULDERS
WITH ROYALTY

When I eventually moved out from the Emslie family hotel into a flat in the centre of Port Elizabeth, things began to calm down as I finally learnt everyone's name and knew in which direction to point my car in order to get to where I was going on time. "On time" was a relative term for some and I soon tired of hearing the phrase "African Time". You have the watches but we have the time, Stuey was another one that was starting to grate as I was often turning up at local clubs only to find that nothing had been organised so, sadly, there weren't any children to coach.

The problem here could be traced back to a huge man by the name of Mella, who wasn't the best when it came to filling my diary with coaching appointments. When I returned to our office, he would greet me like a long lost brother and invite me to join him in his evening ritual of two huge roast chickens he'd picked up from the local Pick n Pay. He ate it so often I wasn't sure whether he'd have a heart attack or actually turn into something that clucked. When I quizzed him about his lack of success in getting me started, he always said they were starting next week. He also said he couldn't understand why I said the word "bollocks" so much. The trouble was he was a charming man and pretty good company so there were many times when I did join him for chicken.

I was sharing my flat with another English pro who had been playing in PE for the previous two season which was useful when it came to local knowledge and things to look out for. He was from the Midlands and, as a young single bloke, was enjoying the trappings of being in a different country. He was hardly ever there, to be honest, a fact that was annoying both me and his girlfriend from home when she regularly phoned to talk to him. As he was rarely there, I chatted to his girlfriend almost as much as I chatted to my wife. One day in the kitchen, he told me how he'd been on a young cricketers' tour to Australia and played Shane Warne with relative ease. Yes, of course you did . . . By November, he'd shacked up with a girl from PE and I think his girlfriend finally gave up the chase.

One of the perks of working at a Test venue is that you are free to roam around and watch the routines of the best players as they prepared and practised as well as see the dressing room rituals and superstitions of some very bizarre men. I was also invited to many functions and saw these stars of cricket enjoy themselves, which they did with relish. The "play hard and party harder" ethic was still prevalent and some of the tales from the away trips were the stuff of legend. It seemed that, once they hit the tarmac for an away match, it was a free for all, well for most of them anyway, although they were all ready to play happy families once they arrived back in PE again, with their wives and girlfriends waiting for them dutifully at the airport.

It was also a chance to meet and watch some of the superstars of the world game who were playing at the time. Although coming towards the end of his illustrious career, Malcolm Marshall, who was playing for Natal gave a masterclass in skill and control while his team mates were going the distance in a Benson and Hedges night game. Watching from the press box, I had one of the best seats in the house and to see the way Marshall moved it both ways and his use of angles was an education in itself, even though the pace of old was in slight decline. His wrist position was second to none and one of the secrets of his unbelievable craft. He finished with four for 20 while EP plundered a huge score that Marshall's Natal side got nowhere near.

One of the highlights for me was meeting Allan Donald and being able to watch him first in the nets and then throughout that winter. It was clear to see why he was one of the absolute superstars of the modern game. A classic action allied to a smooth run up meant he was able to bowl at breakneck speed and completely live up to his nickname of White Lightning. There was little doubt he was the quickest bowler in the world at that stage. Absolute box office. I'd first seen him live a few months previously when I'd done a driving job in the UK for a friend who needed to go to Birmingham for a meeting and, while I waited for him, I did the only sensible thing to do in Birmingham and went to Edgbaston to see Warwickshire play. There, Donald bowled a spell late on the second evening against Derbyshire that was as quick as anything I'd ever witnessed, completely destroying their top order to continue the Bears' relentless charge for the title. It was one of those strange feelings that on one hand you knew you were watching someone utterly world class while, at the same time, feeling almost powerless to comprehend just how good he was compared with you. Sometimes you just need to be brutally honest and admit that, no matter how fit you got or how much you hit the gym and trained, this ability he had was thanks to the big man upstairs. Like it or not, there is truth in the saying that you can't put in what God left out.

What I found perplexing was that when I met him in the nets he was charming and seemed genuinely interested in what I was doing out in PE and how I was enjoying it. After ripping through EP's top order in the first innings, he pulled up after a couple of overs in the second and was strapped to a machine trying to mend his groin in time for the rapidly approaching first Test against England. We sat in the viewing rooms while Kepler steered EP to the safety of a draw and chatted for a while about all things and he was great company. Thankfully, I knew one of the players on the Warwickshire staff so that helped. One thing I have always been good at is not going all fan girl when I meet someone famous and, instead, treat them like normal human beings. One of the other English lads nearly wet himself when he came into the room and just kept going on about how quick Donald was, which I think actually embarrassed the man himself.

We would cross paths a few times that winter and he was always polite and asked me how I was getting on. It's just a shame he was so bloody good and such a shame he wasn't English, as he was about to destroy the English tourists over the coming months.

Although he hadn't broken through to be arguably the greatest player the world has seen, everyone in South Africa was talking about the promise of a young player from Cape Town called Jacques Henry Kallis. So feted was he that when EP played against Western Province in the night series, the ground was full to the brim waiting to see Kallis and the array of stars from down the road in Cape Town. Bowling in the nets before the match, it was good to catch up with Meyrick Pringle who played at Haywards Heath for a few years and also to bowl to the international players they had like Gary Kirsten and Eric Simons and, of course, the brilliant West Indian Desmond Haynes. I was like a kid in a sweetshop, I really was. I listened into all the conversations and tried to glean new ideas that would hopefully improve my game. I still couldn't understand how Pringle could swing the ball like he did, it was ridiculous to watch but bloody impressive.

When the match started, he was too good for the EP players and, despite a late order comeback, the total looked below par. It certainly was as another young player made light of the total. Herschelle Gibbs played some outrageous strokes to smash WP to a comfortable victory, overshadowing Haynes and Kirsten and looking for all money like the maverick superstar he would become. Rumour had it that he might not have been the sharpest tool in the box but who cares when you could bat like he could, and play all the other sports to a ridiculous level for that matter. Another absolute box office cricketer. By the time young master Kallis came to the wicket the job was nearly done and he didn't let anyone down, playing some superb strokes. He just had so much time to see and hit the ball. He'd bowled well, too.

Afterwards, players from both sides mingled in the bar in one of the suites of the Firestone Pavilion. I had to pinch myself to make sure I wasn't dreaming as some of the best players in the world were in the same bar as me and I hadn't even blagged my way in. I chatted with them, listening to the tales of life on the circuit and, of course, where the players were going later on. There was a famous joint just outside Port Elizabeth called The Ranch which, rumour had it, offered more than just the steaks that were on the menu. The visiting players couldn't get there quickly enough. It used to be a common occurrence that if you performed well enough for your club or for the province, someone would take you there as a treat. That night some of the WP boys needed no second invitation

The evening finished in the very early hours as a friend and I walked back across the St George's car park to where our cars were parked. In the distance I could see my lovely Eastern Province sponsored Toyota waiting for me. The strange thing was it didn't seem like we were alone and we soon found out we weren't. On top of my car rested a black Bible while, on my boot, rested a soon to be world-class young cricketer from Cape Town with a very pretty girl somewhere in the vicinity of his legs. I almost felt apologetic in asking if I could have my car back. For some these were the perks of being ridiculously talented and very soon to be ridiculously famous.

17

SLIGHTLY OUT OF
MY DEPTH HERE

There are certain things you'll do in your life that you'll remember as if they were only yesterday and my second match of the season against the so-called students of the University of Port Elizabeth is probably the match that will sit at the top of the tree as far as my cricketing experiences go. It was also the match in which having my head removed from my shoulders became a real possibility.

UPE had spent a lot of money creating a first-class cricket academy where the cream of South Africa's youngsters would go to combine their studies with finishing their cricketing education before, hopefully, being snapped up one of the major provinces. Added to the two teams that would compete in the A League, several of the top EP players would join up to make them even stronger, the last thing you want when your side sits comfortably in middle to lower ranks ability-wise. Seeing the stars you are competing against can sometimes mean you are beaten before you even get your bags into the changing rooms. On rare occasions, you knew you're going to get a major seeing to and there was nothing you can do to avoid it. A bit like trying to take down a Chieftain tank with a pea shooter.

Losing the toss came as no surprise but watching Kepler Wessels and a young Mark Boucher walk down the steps to open the batting did – this was certainly a step up from playing against Bexhill a few weeks earlier. Now young Master Boucher came with the reputation for being a street tough cricketer who was on the verge of breaking into the big time. With some young players, you just knew they were going to make it and, by all accounts and from several respected judges, he fell right into that bracket. And on his journey to the top, he wasn't about to stop and take any interest in people's perceived reputations or worrying in the very slightest about upsetting me. Why should he? His final record in internationals puts him in the highest bracket of keeper / batsmen the world has ever seen.

The game was only a couple of overs old when, much to our delight and genuine surprise, Wessels spooned one up to point and was on his way for hardly any instead of his expected mountain of runs against the clubbies. Sadly for us, he was to be replaced by another of the Eastern Province top four but before too long, he and Boucher had a mix-up running between the wickets and both ended up at the same end while we happily took the bails off at the other. Now, if you want to carry on living, the normal thing to do in this situation is to agree that the experienced old pro with plenty of first class runs was probably right all along and then you turn around and slowly walk off. But that wasn't Mr Boucher's way. He rested firmly on his bat handle knowing full well that he was safe and that it was his partner who had to head for the pavilion. One man's rather gutsy is another man's rather stupid, they say and, as the shock of what had happened was dying down, I decided to mention that it'd be a good idea for him to bat for as long as he could, just so he could avoid explaining to Kepler and his mates what he'd just done. A fair point, I thought, but when Boucher replied with a full bouquet of very rude words all joined together to form a sentence of sorts, I realised he might not have been too impressed with my opinion.

Better was to follow a couple of overs later when Mr Boucher generously nicked me straight into the big hands of second slip, who did well to cling on to leave them in some trouble. As he walked past me I thought a rueful grin might be enough, only to be met with a very rude word. To be fair, I've been called rude words like that before but for Boucher to work out what many other batsmen already thought of me in only 6.2 overs was impressive indeed.

Although wickets kept falling at regular intervals, Graham Grace, who would come and join me at East Grinstead the following season, and a superb player called Greg Miller, who was one of those talented gits who could play pro sport at either cricket or rugby, both got some runs to make the total somewhat easier to defend. As the innings entered its final phase, Brett Schultz came out to bat at number 11. Not a man renowned for his batting prowess, he swatted my first two balls for four before I decided that enough was enough and banged one in short which he obligingly hit straight up in the air. I'd had a pretty good day, I'd bowled quickly on a bouncy pitch, hit the bat hard and picked up four wickets for not many so, by rights, my teammates should have been pretty happy with the performance of their new recruit. But not a bit of it. They sat sullenly in the changing room looking like they'd just seen the grim reaper. Maybe they were trying to tell me something I didn't know. Now I'd met Brett Schultz a few times before but had never seen him bowl -though I'd heard he was more than quick – and, as far as my new team mates were concerned, I'd just made him angry by getting him out third ball. Slightly harsh, I thought.

Schultz was a big man who had been suffering after another knee operation and seeing him limber up I could only imagine the stress they went through his joints each time he ran up to bowl. All the players seemed to have a tale to tell about their duels with him and now it was my turn to witness the main event from the safety of the pavilion. His first two balls weren't too bad, quick but nothing outrageous, and then, oh fuck, fuck, fuckity, fuck fuck, the sudden realisation that this bloke is so unbelievably quick it's scary. That's all my tiny little mind could muster. There's now the real possibility that I'm going to die sometime in the next 30 overs. How on earth am I going to play this without serious damage to my health? Wicketkeeper Boucher, standing at least 25 yards back, could only watch helplessly as the fourth ball sailed over his head for four byes.

Now I'd hoped that my team mates could survive long enough for me to face something a lot slower when it was my turn to bat. No such luck as our opener is hit so hard on the helmet that he fell on his stumps and had to be carried off. Not great for your heart rate, in all honesty. I thought maybe I could offer to take him to hospital and get myself out of the firing line, but no such luck. Still, we had some of EP's best youngsters including Ashwell Prince to come and they'd save me. Surely. Not today they wouldn't as they all came and went quicker than you could say "Time to call the ambulance".

My move to the calmness of the changing room didn't help and its silent torment resembled something out of the Gladiator movie when all of the fighters knew they were facing certain death. My hopeless search for as much padding as I could muster helped a little and I ended up wrapping two towels around my chest and inner thighs for added protection. One kind team mate lent me his chest guard as it wasn't too sweaty after his ineffective two-ball marathon. I looked like the Michelin Man as I waited on the pavilion bench. If mobile phones had existed for all and sundry at the time, this was the moment you would have phoned home to tell your wife you loved her and explained where the life insurance policy was kept as you may well be killed sometime in the next ten minutes.

With the fall of the sixth wicket, my wait was over. Now get into line Stuart, don't show them that you're shitting yourself, even though you might be and, for god's sake try to watch the ball. It's only 90-plus miles an hour on a really bouncy pitch. As I took guard I tried to look like nothing was worrying me, in the way Mark Waugh would do it, the only trouble being he was slightly better than me. As I looked about, the slips and close catchers weren't actually that close, and there were lots of them and they were miles away. Actually they were in another postcode they were that far away. I could still hear Mark Boucher offering his opinion, but this didn't seem like the day to turn around and have a go back. The first ball came and went without much involvement from me, to be honest, as I had no idea what happened because I honestly didn't see it at all. The observers would have seen me casually play inside the line while the ball thudded into the keeper's gloves. Despite the fact that I know how to hold a bat, I'd suddenly realised that I was in such deep shit not even gallows humour could help me now. Then, suddenly, it all clicked and my natural reactions took over. The second ball was short and my feet went back and across, my bat came down dead straight and the perfect backwards defensive was achieved as the ball rolled back towards the bowler. Les Lenham would have been proud but I was just thrilled because that was the end of the over, meaning I could try to get out at the other end and at least stay alive.

No such luck and I prepared to face another Schultz over. As he was both left armed and ludicrously quick, there was nowhere for me to get out of the way, especially as he could swing the ball in towards you. You couldn't even run for cover. Still, I was surviving. The next ball flew at my head and my natural reaction was to try and hook it which was just plain stupid as I was so late on it that it hit the bat before I'd really moved and flew for four over the slips who, quite rightly, laughed. Not quite how the hook shot was played in the coaching demos, if I'm honest. The next ball was worse, swinging back and hitting me in the ribs. I tried to make out it didn't hurt but wasn't kidding anyone. I was down on my knees and checking that the ball hadn't actually gone straight through me and come out the other side of my body. Not even a towel and a chest pad could save me. The umpire told me to take my time and I took him at his word. I asked if I could come back next week to which one of the UPE lads informed me that I'd still be shit then. He might well have been right.

When I finally got back and took guard again, the best thing happened, I got a nice juicy outside edge and I was about to be put out of my misery. I'm out but I'm still alive, I thought, before Boucher and first slip left it for each other and it flew for four. Schultz went nuts and I felt like joining him. I've never sledged anyone for dropping me but this seemed a good place to start. I got a big inside edge to the next ball that sped away into the deserted outfield so there was an easy three which, best of all, would have got me away from the strike but my batting partner Chris Andrews had other ideas and, after running the second, threw himself to the floor as if he'd been shot by a sniper perched in the trees. Braveheart indeed.

Finally, in the following over the inevitable happened when Schultz swung one in so late that it removed both middle and leg stumps, a first for me. I'd scored 17 before but never like this. I walked off and sat down in the changing room trying to get my head around what I'd just been through. I had what looked like a shark-sized love bite on my ribs and the realisation that Schultz was simply quick enough to kill me if the ball had hit me in the wrong place. I knew I was pretty quick when it all clicked but this was simply top draw pace and to face it was a mixture of bloody exciting and bloody terrifying.

To cap it all, when the after-game rituals were over, the man himself stormed into our changing rooms and demanded that I join him on a night out and who was I to refuse? To Cadillac Jacks nightclub we went and legless we got. I'd heard the man was a legend and I wasn't disappointed.

18

CANE AND COKE
WITH EVERYTHING

As a visitor to South Africa, I tried hard to fit in with its customs and not claim the way we did things back in the UK was any better. For me that meant listening to what people said and soaking up as much information as possible. I was delighted to eat, sleep and drink cricket with as many different people as I could.

Saturday nights after matches would include the regular fines meetings where most things that happened during the match were only an excuse to drink as much Castle lager as you could and it was frowned upon if you decided you needed to be somewhere else. The whole club culture was one to be admired. Thankfully there were never any incidents akin to the famous Michael Clarke/Simon Katich stand off and some of the trumped up charges laid at people's doors were hilarious. And it was after matches that you were really able to witness the different types of lives people were living.

One night I was taken to a shebean which is, I guess, a drinking hole in the middle of the township. I was made incredibly welcome and, although completely out of my comfort zone, it was one of the most memorable nights of my trip. The people and their sense of community were so important to each other and it showed that money and material items really only have so much going for them. Drink flowed freely all night and stories were told about the days before the elections and what life had been like during apartheid to the extent that you wondered how on earth there hadn't been civil war in South Africa. It was a credit to the people that they saw the future as a positive chance to change things for the next generations. I'd entered as a slightly nervous English tourist and left in utter amazement at how these people lived and yet always looked so cheerful.

In sharp contrast, a night at Port Elizabeth Cricket Club was like seeing things from the other side of the fence with people who had enjoyed the benefit of going to better schools and universities, been able to travel overseas and live what would be considered a normal, first world existence. This isn't meant as a slur, just an obvious deduction. It was clear that back in 1995 the older generation were desperately unsure about what the future had in store for them and the doom mongers among them had little faith in South Africa's future. This applied as much to the future of cricket as it did to the state of the economy. The tales of club life and the brilliant players who graced the scene for years was always entertaining and made me grateful that, for a short while, I was part of this rich tapestry. As with most things though, the whole experiences are made worthwhile by the friends that you make and, with PECC captain Murray Brown, I made a friend for life. Although very different people, we hit it off like a house on fire and are still best mates more than two decades later. He's a brilliant bloke and has been an amazing friend over the years. The best thing was that I only ever bowled at him only once during a match, got him out third ball and still take great pleasure in reminding him about it all these years later. Eternal bragging rights if you like. In fairness, PECC were national club champions and had one hell of a team made up of mainly provincial and Springbok players and if you performed well against them, you genuinely could fancy your chances against any professional side. My five-for in my first match against them still stands out as one of my proudest feats.

The match against Union CC gave me the chance to meet James Carse, an outright quick bowler in his pomp who had spells in county cricket at Northants. Ending up in a small group that went back to his house, you suddenly realised that the lives of the white South Africans had, until very recently, involved National Service, which, to a nice middle class boy from Sussex, was a fairly daunting thought.

Right then Stu, you're not going to college where you can spend too much of your time failing to chat up most of the girls on the secretarial courses, you're going to be packed off to places like Angola or Mozambique instead, where you're going to be shot at several times a week. Errrrr? You can stick that thought somewhere else thank you very much.

That however was a reality for thousands of young men my age and the tales that Carse told me made my hairs stand on end. If I'd been through what he had been through, I would have no doubt consumed the same amount of cane and coke that he did. Even though he was coming towards the end of his long playing days and had appeared to play for almost every club in Port Elizabeth, he could still hit the bat hard and I'd have loved to have seen him bowl during his prime, although preferably not with a bat in my hand.

It wasn't only the standard of cricket that appealed to me, it was soaking up knowledge from internationals down to club players, because they too had to survive and prosper in this league and that took skill and guts. As with everything in life, there were some chancers and some who talked a great game, but the culture was such that they soon got weeded out and, without trying to sound too sentimental, if I was able to gain the respect of some of these blokes, both on and off the cricket field, then that was more than enough for me.

After every weekend, in a world before the Internet and cricket websites, you would hunt down a copy of the Eastern Province Herald newspaper and see how all the players and all the teams had got on. Club cricket had a massive write up and the goal was always to make it into the top ten performances, which I did a few times that season. The list always including some big names, so it was always pleasing to see yours alongside theirs. Thankfully, many years earlier, some bright spark told me to start a scrapbook with all the cuttings from wherever I played and did well and it has proved more than worthwhile. Proof for the grandchildren that grandpa wasn't too bad back in the day.

19

I WISH IT COULD BE
CHRISTMAS EVERY DAY

As the festive season approached, the whole of Port Elizabeth was starting to prepare itself for the arrival of the touring England team for the fourth Test match, due to start on Boxing Day. I'd been fortunate that the Christmas coaching clinics we'd run at Grey High School had been profitable and so when Jacky came out for a long holiday we were able to disappear down the stunning Garden Route on our way to the beautiful city of Cape Town. To see her face when we reached its outskirts was a picture in itself as she instantly fell in love with the place. We were both happy to play Tommy Tourist for a few days before heading back to PE to prepare for the invasion of Mike Atherton's side and the large crowds that were expected.

For the first time, I'd been able to witness the huge logistical challenge that presented itself involving tickets, stewarding, television requirements and making sure the ground was in peak condition. Watching the Castle lager trucks bring the beer in for day one alone was a sight to see as they stocked all the bars and hospitality boxes. My main job was to be somewhat more appealing as I was assigned to bowl at both the English and South African players at the nets on Christmas Day and then on each morning of the match. Actually, I had to be available pretty much all of the time if players not in the starting XIs or those arriving for the one-day series that followed the Test series fancied a hit.

The Test match also meant the arrival of the Sky TV commentary team which was already starting to resemble a legends' gallery with my hero Mr Gower among their number. I'd given myself a good talking too about trying to stay calm if I actually got to meet the great man after all these years of total and utter adoration.

As I opened my curtains in my flat on Christmas Day morning, I was genuinely more excited about the upcoming events than I had been since I was about seven years old hoping that Santa would bring me something Thunderbirds related or a James Bond Dinky toy. I was about to bowl at the cream of the country's batsmen and see, first hand, just how much better than me they actually were. Hopefully I wouldn't embarrass myself and be asked to leave the net, which had happened before to other bowlers. As I pulled into the St George's car park, the nets were packed with spectators and the camera crews from both Sky and the African satellite broadcaster Supersport. I had to fight my way through to meet England tour manager John Barclay who I knew well from several coaching courses with Sussex. John is arguably the nicest bloke ever known to humanity, but he still gave me goose bumps when he told me that some net bowlers at the previous Test in Durban had been asked to leave after about ten balls each. No pressure I thought, bowl like a dick, get smashed around by the

England players and then be asked to bugger off for essentially being shite, all in front of Charles Colvile and the Sky TV crew.

When all the important players had arrived, it became clear that the dear old national side didn't seem a particularly happy bunch and that the tensions between the coaching staff and the cricketers was near boiling point. The coach Ray Illingworth had brought in some of his peers to assist him during the tour and it was clear that the current crop of players thought they were from another, bygone era. I just got my head down, spoke to players who fancied a chat and tried not to bowl any pies. All along, John Barclay kept giving me the thumbs up which I hope meant I was doing well enough to stay at the party. Mike Atherton, Alec Stewart and Graham Thorpe were the first three up and I was thrilled I bowled well to them, especially Atherton who I thought was a national treasure. The commotion though was at the bowling end of the nets where Devon Malcolm and bowling coach Peter Lever had starting rucking and it wasn't long before the big fast bowler decided he'd had enough and left the session early.

Sure enough, after about 20 minutes, two young bowlers who played at United CC were asked to leave the nets and so at least I wasn't the first to get the chop. Through the whole morning, I have to say that I thought Ray Illingworth was a really nice bloke and I spent quite a lot of time talking to him while waiting my turn to bowl. He was polite and interested in what I was doing in Port Elizabeth. When he asked me what county I was at, he seemed genuinely surprised when I told him I was a clubbie but if he wanted to find me a county that would be very decent of him!

The two players I was keenest to bowl at were Robin Smith and Graeme Hick. Smith simply to see if he could unleash one of his famous square cuts to something I'd offer up and when I bowled one as quickly as I could, short and outside off stump, he duly obliged by getting on one knee and smashing it. I was thrilled. John Barclay had been watching and asked whether I'd done it on purpose. I couldn't lie so I said that I had but it had been well worth it. In his lovely Old Etonian accent, he kept telling me: "Stuart, these are the England players, you really are doing so well, so well."

For me, as with most cricket followers around the globe, Graeme Hick was the great unanswered enigma of our time. Why had someone with so much talent and so much time to hit the ball not made a better fist of a Test career that was now into its fifth or sixth year? He'd been dropped more times than anyone cared to remember and, even though he'd cemented his place in this England side, you still felt that it was only a matter of time before the axe fell again. Now I had a brief chance to see first-hand what he was like up close and witness how he destroyed county bowlers for a pastime. To be honest, to start with I was fairly underwhelmed as he didn't seem to have the time to hit it that, say, an Alec Stewart had or the really tight technique of Mike Atherton. That's not to say he wasn't a brilliant player and, the one time I drifted onto his pads, he flicked the ball with a grace and ease that only the lucky few can manage. The ball flew out of the nets and didn't appear to want to come down. It went absolutely miles and was one of those hits that made everyone stop what they were doing to see just how far it was going to go. For me, I'd been hit out of a cricket ground many times before, but this was the first time I'd actually been hit into one as the ball finally landed on the St George's Park outfield. They should have called NASA it went so high.

As the long session drew to a close and I prepared to head off, I had the dubious honour of having lots of young children thrust their bats and autograph books in my direction. What do I do? Ask them if they really want some illegible squiggle on their Gray Nicolls and Slazengers from the less than hugely well-known opening bowler from East Grinstead? Or do I just look like I belong and sign away, knowing that it might be the only time this is going to happen? So, sure enough, I signed away, trying to look like I did this sort of thing all the time. And, let's not kid ourselves here, I loved every minute of it.

The saddest thing was when I saw Jacky waiting for me outside the nets. I had a big smile on my face and was looking pretty pleased with myself but I could see she'd been crying. When I asked her why, she said that, as she'd been watching with all the other spectators, lots of them had asked which county I played at and that she thought I didn't look out of place. I thought she'd been crying because I'd been crap but, actually, she'd been crying because she didn't think it was fair. Sometimes I guess life just isn't. . .

20

BETTER NOT TELL THE INSURANCE MAN

As the morning of the Test match finally arrived, all the planning worries came to end as two teams, the umpires and thousands of spectators turned up to witness the first ball at 10.30 on Boxing Day morning. I'd bowled at the England players for an hour before play and was pleased I'd been judged good enough to return while some others had failed to get the invitation. To see the faces of the players not selected was interesting, to say the least, and Darren Gough had a face like thunder all morning when he found out about his omission. Every day after nets I was invited back by Mr Illingworth for a drink in the dressing room area but I never stayed too long as I felt like a bit of an intruder waiting for security to finally realise who I was and eject me.

The start of the match also meant the entrance of the players' wives and families and, in some cases, entourages. The England group were watching from the Firestone pavilion while the South Africans were in the viewing area next door to our offices and it seemed that, for five hot days in Port Elizabeth, this was the place to be as more famous cricketers than I ever dared hope to see came through to watch and have a chat with someone of equally noteworthy status.

The food on offer for all to enjoy was excellent – I'm sure it was of a much higher standard than that on offer in the hospitality boxes around the ground – so I was rolling about like a pig in a blanket. It was interesting to see which of the wives acted as mother hen of the group, protecting the wives and girlfriends of the younger players who'd just made the side, and also which wives clearly didn't have much time for each other, no doubt due to an altercation between their husbands, and gave each other serious daggers every day.

I was lucky enough to see so many things for myself before being summoned to go and bowl to someone either out of form or waiting to go in to bat, which sometimes buggered up my enjoyment of the food on offer. As the one-day players had arrived, every afternoon was a lengthy net session with the fun of watching Mark Ramprakash destroy everything that was served up to him in a session they called "deluxe hitting" where batsmen were told to hit every ball for six or four as if you were at the end of a one-day innings. I quickly worked out not to get in his net as he belted Devon Malcolm with ridiculous ease. I have to say that, in an era before laptop analysis and data logging, the coaches in the England party didn't seem to offer any real nuggets of wisdom to the players and maybe that was the problem as they were hammered out of sight when the series actually started.

On the other hand, and under Bob Woolmer's direction, the South African's seemed far more structured and happy to use all the latest tools and TV gadgets that 1995 had to offer. Every player was monitored and nothing was left to chance in order to get a slight advantage over the opposition. It also gave me the chance to bowl next to Allan Donald who, if I remember correctly, seemed to get the ball to the other end slightly quicker than I did. To watch him stretch and loosen up was both interesting and sickening at the same time as, for a bloke who is only a couple of months older than me, he was so supple that he could get into all sorts of stretching positions that would have sent me to the chiropractor. Ridiculously flexible, it surely helped him bowl so effortlessly quickly day after day. Watching that talent stand next to you at first hand, you realised that god had been very kind to AA Donald. Hansie Cronje seemed to be the most intense man I'd ever met and it wouldn't really be telling tales to say that Daryll Cullinan didn't seem to be the most popular member of the squad. The bowlers all seemed to give a little bit more effort and bowl somewhat shorter of a length when he went into the nets. The thing was that he was such a talented bloke with so much time to play the ball that I'm not sure he actually realised.

One of the things we had to do was to be on hand to help out if needed and this was never a problem if it meant helping get some items to the boxes or take some of the players' wives to the nearby shopping mall or back to the hotel in Summerstrand. What it didn't say in the job description was pushing Dominic Cork's baby up and down the hallway in a pram while a rather unhappy Mrs Cork went to fetch something she'd forgotten from the hospitality box. Still I think she did the same to her husband after the end of each day's play.

Perhaps the highlight came as the second day ended and Dave Emslie asked if I could take some people back to the hotel. Not a problem, I thought, and I was pleasantly surprised to see the Sky TV commentators Mark Nicholas and the legend that is Bob

Willis waiting by the office doors. Both extremely pleasant blokes, we chatted about various things as we walked to the car when, all of a sudden, a certain Mr I T Botham joined us for the journey. As I drove away from the ground with my three very important passengers, I couldn't help but recall that conversation I had with a certain insurance company a couple of years earlier. Thankfully the insurance for this journey was taken care of by the Eastern Province Cricket Board so I didn't feel compelled to phone up and change my policy details. But I really did have Ian Botham in my car. All I needed to do now was to go and find Elvis, which might have proved somewhat harder.

21

MEETING A PROPER ICON

The second half of the season passed by as a longer version of a two-week holiday where you think you'll be away for ages and then, before you know it, you're packing up and getting ready to say your goodbyes and hit the airport.

I came across a young and raw Nantie Hayward while coaching at the UPE nets one morning and was seriously impressed by how quickly and aggressively he bowled. At the start of his career, his action had the hint of a throw which was probably due to the amount of baseball he used to play but it was smoothed out in no time and the result was a lad with the ability to bowl at breakneck speed and who would soon challenge Brett Schultz and Allan Donald as the quickest in the land. Worse was to follow as he he was playing for Uitenhage in the league and we had them in the next round of fixtures.

As Hayward was a proper slogger and used to heave across the line batting at No 11, I thought I'd keep quiet when he stood there trying to carve me into the next town, but some of our players weren't so thoughtful with their advice and, boy, did he make them pay. Some of their natural colour had drained from their faces as they saw him steaming in and reaching speeds that would have scared the most able, especially on a wicket that wasn't the best. We were all out quickly and Hayward proved yet again that top draw pace always sorts out the men from the boys. It was fair to say that he wasn't the most charming of men, but that wouldn't stop plenty of provinces and counties seeking out his services over the following years as pace like his was a rare commodity indeed and people were always willing to put up with quite of lot of baggage if you can get to around 150kph on the speed gun.

By the end of January, the ODI series was coming to a close and, when the teams returned to Port Elizabeth for the last of a seven-match series, South Africa had shattered England's World Cup 1996 ambitions by hammering the tourists into submission, leaving them looking like a tired and battered group of men desperately in need of a tactical rethink on one hand, and a return flight home on the other.

To be honest, back then, as soon as a World Cup appeared on the horizon, England's planning seemed to become muddled. There were constant changes to the side and no one was really clear as to what their roles actually were. Some of the selection decisions were hard to understand and, sadly, the results and performances made for dismal reading. At the start, the experts were predicting a fairly comfortable England series win, but it soon became clear Hansie Cronje's men held all the trump cards and were streets ahead of England in all departments and showed it in almost every match, taking a five-one lead going into the match at St George's Park.

The final nails in England's winter tour were being knocked in over by over, and even bowling at the nets pre-match was not the experience it had been even a few weeks earlier as the players appeared to have no appetite for the fight after so many beatings and harsh column inches from the media. Most were dreaming of landing at Heathrow as soon as humanly possible.

From a personal point of view, I had met so many famous people over the previous few weeks that the thought of adding another one to the list didn't worry me too much. However, when that one extra person happens to be the South African president, Nelson Mandela, then that's something that makes your hairs stand on end. We had heard a rumour he might be attending and it wasn't until the morning of the match that Dave Emslie asked me whether I'd like to meet Mandela – or my boyhood hero David Gower. Tongue-in-check I replied that I'd love to meet Gower, so he stopped and asked, in his sternest boss voice, whether I would like to rethink my answer. When I realised there was a chance I might meet Mandela, I forgot about not bowling like a complete tool to the England players that morning and wondered what it would be like to meet probably the greatest and certainly the most famous statesmen in the world.

To try to comprehend what he'd been through before and after his imprisonment was impossible, yet he'd taken on the seemingly impossible task of uniting the vastly different parts of South Africa with skill and huge patience. I'd been to both Mandela concerts at Wembley Stadium and heard him speak at the second after his release so to get the chance to stand next to him was, in short, a thrill. With the game looking like another comfortable win for South African, the noise of the crowd reached fever pitch amid reports that Mandela was on his way from the airport. As I was already in the EP offices, I knew that he would have to come close to where we were and so I loitered around trying to look important and kept my fingers crossed.

To see the motorcades pull up to the pavilion steps was completely surreal and then, after the bodyguards had made sure everything was safe, the great man along with Dr Ali Bacher entered the building. Dave Emslie was his charming self as usual as he spoke to the president and introduced him to the various cricketing dignitaries from the ICC and EP Cricket and then he ushered him through towards our offices. In a flash, amazingly, I was being introduced to Nelson Mandela and I shook his hand. He listened politely as I told him what I'd been doing in the townships and in the development programme. What I found most bizarre was that I was standing chatting to arguably the most most famous and instantly recognisable man on the planet. Not even the biggest Hollywood royalty could match Nelson Mandela.

The other thing that makes you think is when you catch a glimpse inside the bodyguards' jackets and realise they are packing some serious armoury and that, if it came to it, those weapons would need to come out and the bodyguards would do what was necessary in order to protect the president. Half reassuring and half ridiculously scary, if I'm honest.

As the line finished and Mandela made his way to the privacy of his box, the match wound down before the crowd realised he was inside the ground and the fanfare began. To see such a reaction was priceless and made you realise how different it was when, back home in the UK, John Major got abuse for bunking off from his day job to watch a Test match, when surely there were more pressing things for a Prime Minister to be doing.

When the game finished, and England had finally been beaten 6-1, the players and officials from both sides lined up to meet the president striding out to the middle with his South African cricket blazer on, to more noise than I had ever heard at a cricket ground before, and probably ever will again. Occasionally you are lucky enough to have some moments in your life when you just happen to be in the right place at the right time to capture the insanity of it all. This was one such day, a day I will never forget.

When the action was finally over and the ground started to return to normal, all the officials and staff made their way to the bar at Castle Corner and had what can only be described as a fairly major party. Returning to my flat later, I called Jacky and greeted her in my best pissed up tone with: "Now, you're never going to guess who I met today. . ."

22

SORRY SON, TIME TO GO HOME

All good things must come to an end, as they say, and my first season as a fully paid up overseas professional in Port Elizabeth was certainly one that fell into that category. The last few weeks went quickly and, before I knew it, I was shaking the hands and saying farewell and good luck with way too many people who were actually now my friends. All done and dusted and heading to the airport before I realised it was over.

Before the short drive to the airport, I had been asked to make a speech about my experiences to the ladies and gentlemen of the Port Elizabeth Social Club which was akin to speaking to a SAGA meeting in your local village hall. I'd heard they were a tough audience and that some previous speakers had been met by a wall of silence so, with this potentially in store for me, I came armed with a few stories and some stolen jokes, hoping they'd feel sorry for an Englishman in South Africa and go easy on me. I'm not quite sure they got my sarcastic sense of humour but they clapped in all the right places and, according to the organisers, laughed a hell of a lot more than they had for a few meetings where the speakers had a lot more cricketing credibility than I did. "Why are England so pathetically bad at cricket," was one of the questions from the floor. I looked at my watch and then replied by looking at the host and asking how much time I had to answer before last orders at the bar. They appreciated my honesty on lots of subjects and I left with a voucher to spend at a local restaurant and some fine wine which, in reality, was about as useful as a chocolate teapot as I was leaving in a couple of days and don't really like wine so Dave Emslie and his wife Sandra ended up doing quite well out of me that night.

When I returned to the offices at St George's the next morning I was treated as some sort of celebrity for surviving and conquering the baying mob of senior citizens and, to my amazement, they'd asked if I could come to talk again in a couple of months. Sadly, that was not likely to happen and, if it did, it was going to cost a hell of a lot more to get me there than it did last time.

The final game of the season against Old Grey finished in a damp affair as the rain ruined any prospects of play after lunch and so all that was left to do was have a few drinks with the opposition and then head back to into town. Sad as it was for me to end in such a way, it was worse for young Nigel Brouwers, the talented all rounder who was linked with the EP squad. We had had a bet running the whole season that if he scored a hundred in the league then I'd give him my Sussex tracksuit which he'd been trying to get his grubby hands on from the day I'd arrived. For my part, if he didn't get to three figures, then he had to run three laps of the ground completely naked. Seemed a fair bet to me. When he edged behind for another pretty 20, most of the players didn't know whether to laugh of cry and, as all the Old Grey team knew he only had one chance left, they weren't shy in letting Nigel know what awaited him if he failed. So, when the stumps were finally pulled from the ground with the rain streaming down, the sight of big Nigel walking out onto the oval wrapped in just a towel caused great amusement to all the spectators and, true to form, he dropped it to the floor and started jogging with all his glory on show. Top lad Nigel, as many would have bolted pretty quickly to avoid the embarrassment. Did I give him the tracksuit? Of course I didn't!

Gelvandale put on a lunchtime *braai* for me the following day to thank me for my efforts during the season which, for a club with absolutely no money, was a lovely gesture and various club officials said some very flattering things which touched me greatly. They were superb people and looked after me with great warmth and as a club they have continued to produce many players for the province and a couple have even played for South Africa as they continue to be a force in the region.

My last morning at the offices in Park Drive, Port Elizabeth was a mixture of sadness and pride and again Dave Emslie said some lovely things about me as a player, coach and, most importantly to me, as a person and, to be honest, I nearly lost it for a moment. For me, he remains probably the best person I have ever worked for and there was nothing I wouldn't have done for him. Quite simply, he was a brilliant man. He'd given me the chance of a lifetime, and I'd done my best to grab it with both hands. I'd had the chance to play against some true international stars and many, many superb players. To be able to eat, sleep and drink top level cricket and sport was a chance that is not afforded to many people. I had held my own and didn't let East Grinstead, Sussex or England down. In many ways, it was six months that would shape my future outlook greatly and, for that, I will be eternally grateful and forever thankful.

The flight home took even longer than the one out and, by the time I arrived in Heathrow, I'd been travelling for nearly two days after a long stop off in Athens, which is probably a punishment of sorts for being a cheapskate on the plane tickets. When the wheels touched down, there was a uniformed groan when everyone saw the crappy weather conditions we had come back to and, if ever there was a reminder that I was back in the UK, it was to watch it piss down with rain while we sat in traffic on the M25. You've got to love England.

23

IT WAS THE SUMMER
OF '96

When I look back to the summer of 1996 what instantly springs to mind is that England got annoying close to actually winning something at football for the first and probably only time in my life. Gazza's wonder goal against Scotland followed by the perfect performance against the Dutch meant the whole nation went completely mad for Euro 96, only to be let down when, as usual, we lost to the Germans on penalties. In all honesty, I've never forgiven Gareth Southgate. Oasis was the band on everyone's CD player culminating in their two, massive sold out concerts at Knebworth, with every person on earth seeming to sing Wonderwall at every given opportunity before the Spice Girls stormed to the top of the charts, launching the gruesomely packaged girl power revolution for any female under 14.

For yours truly, there were a few advantages of returning to the UK before the fun started in early 1996 but in truth I can't really think of too many other than seeing Jacky. The cat had also lost the plot and needing counselling. It was freezing, the boiler had as good as blown up and I was missing the South African sunshine. Still, I'd returned home fitter and stronger, with a proper set of fast bowler's shoulders and a new-found confidence in my improvements which I was keen to show off once the action started again in late April.

The reaction to my return home from my African adventure was, to be fair, rather underwhelming. Now I wasn't expecting an open top bus ride or ticker tape parade or anything like that but if you sit down with a group of cricketers you play with week in, week out you might expect them to ask you something more detailed than "Did you have a nice time"? Apart from a couple of mates, that's pretty much all I got and, not for the first time, I got to thinking that most people aren't that interested in what other people do. They hope you've had a good time, been safe, taken a few photos and then returned home to continue living your life, just like everyone else. But I'd done some things I thought were worth talking about – I'd met Nelson Mandela and played with the England and South African squads but I didn't get much more than "Oh, that's nice." Nothing as queer as folk, I thought.

I had a pleasant surprise on my return to Hove when I was offered a season-long job on decent money which meant I'd gone from one professional club straight to another which was an improvement on trying to make ends meet as a jobbing coach-come-player.

I was to carry on coaching as usual, and would supplement my income by working in the marketing department. Peter Moores soon saw I was around and, before long, he managed to persuade the various people that it would be highly beneficial to the club if I was to bowl in the nets before matches and at just about every practice as the Sussex roadshow went around the county. The marketing manager didn't even know I played cricket so, for him, it came as quite a shock. In truth, I was nearly flogged to death by all and sundry who spent the summer arguing about where I was supposed to be and who was supposed to be paying my salary. My only request was that I got Saturdays off to play for East Grinstead and that I was allowed to play for MCC when my fixtures came up. With everything agreed, the pleasure I felt from walking off with so much branded clothing was sinful, and I got to drive a shiny new sponsored car for most of the summer as I looked every bit the player I wished I was. The regular money plus generous expenses allowed my bank account to finally come off life support and made me wonder where the DR letters had gone every time I went to the cashpoint.

Before leaving Port Elizabeth, I'd arranged for Graham Grace to come to England as our overseas player for the season. Having played against him in the leagues I knew he was a bloody good batsman and would be a superb lad around the club. The only problem was that he had a new girlfriend and found it hard to say goodbye to the lovely Cindy for six months. In the days before digital messaging, they would send each other the longest love letters I'd ever seen. I'd sorted the deal out with his parents and, in early April, he appeared at the airport looking bloody cheerful to start a fruitful career playing as a professional.

The first task was to show him where everything was and then to take him up to the club and meet some of the players. After that, I took him back to the house he was going to live in during his stay and headed home. I expected to see him again later the next day but got rather a shock when there was a loud knock on my front door at 6am. Standing there, in his running gear, was our new signing, keen to go out jogging with me. After swearing at him several times, I brought him inside and introduced him to Sky Sports while explaining that the sun doesn't get up as early as it does in Africa and turned to go back to bed. Graham, though, looked like a little lost boy and I was soon pounding the streets with him before driving to Hove for work. When the 106-page letters from Cindy started arriving on a regular basis, thankfully Graham had less interest in being at my front door at such a ridiculous time of the morning.

24

INDIAN SUMMER ONLY IT'S MAY

There are times when you wonder what it must be like to be so unbelievably famous that you're not able to walk down the street without being hounded by fans or having the shirt ripped off your back as some sort of bizarre piece of memorabilia. In the early summer of 1996, I somehow managed to be in the company of Sachin Tendulkar for a few days in May and got to understand what it must have been like to have been one of the Beatles. It also gave me a bird's eye view of the fine lines between talent, good fortune and luck and to be around those who have managed to fall the right side of that line.

When you bowled at players as much as I did, it can become like any job on a day-to-day basis. What started out as a thrill to bowl to full time pros and test yourself against them could become a mixture of realising that you're a glorified bowling machine, only one that got tired and had sore shins and back, and, on the other hand, wondering how on earth some of these players received a monthly cheque for playing cricket. That, I suppose, is all part of the layer cake, where there is almost a team within a team and, even at professional level just like at a club, there is a huge difference between the players at the top of the tree and those a bit further down. However, despite my occasional lethargy, when the players walking into the nets are treated like gods in a country of more than a billion people, then there is understandably more a spring in your step. And when one of their number is SR Tendulkar, destined to become one of the greatest ever to play the game, then that is the stuff of dreams, even to a bloke who's married and in his late twenties.

There was a good crowd watching, all waiting for a glimpse of their heroes and ready to shout and scream when they saw a good shot. The youngsters in the side like Ganguly and Dravid would become legends in their own right, but it was Tendulkar was the name on everyone's lips since he entered the harsh world of international cricket. In all honesty, he was simply magnificent, his feet movement, balance and power were breathtaking. You knew this was a man who was on a far higher plain than the others. Sheer unadulterated class, nothing more, nothing less. I felt like he knew where the ball was going to pitch before I'd even bowled it and therefore he'd decided where the ball was headed before I'd actually realised it. It's a strange feeling that, even though you aren't playing in a match, you still want to get the top players out even though you don't mind serving one up so the superstars can produce one of their trademark strokes. It's never quite so bad when someone like Tendulkar or Mark Waugh puts a decent ball outside off stump effortlessly through mid wicket. I wasn't in a hurry to advise them that they ought to play straighter and hit the ball in the V. You just pick the ball up, walk back to the top of the net and wait until it's your turn to have another go. You are, after all, bowling at a genius and that doesn't happen very often, for anyone.

Halfway through his net, the strangest thing happened when, after sending another one down the other end and hoping not to be embarrassed, the normally prolific Sachin made a rare error and nicked it to where second slip would have been standing. As you can imagine, I had the biggest smile on my face akin to getting a winning lottery ticket. At the top of the net stood Bill Athey, the former England opener who was finishing his career at Hove and due to play in the game the following day. "Single to third man, Simmo," he chuckled. Advising him that the rule of the nets was that every bowler has at least 19 fielders, he replied in his Yorkshire accent, "Simmo, you're bowling to Sachin Tendulkar, even with 19 fielders I'm still not giving you two slips. Like I said, single to third man, but well bowled, mate."

After the little maestro had thanked all the bowlers he departed and went to sign what appeared to be countless autographs. The next batter in was Mohammad Azharuddin who, without wanting to get my unknown effigy burnt in every city in India, seemed even better than the previous incumbent, if that were actually possible. He was simply unbelievable and, for the first time ever in a net session, I felt almost powerless to know where to bowl. Everything was whipped through the on side no matter where you bowled it and, maddening though it was, I would have needed every one of those 19 fielders to protect the boundary. I guess his involvement in the match fixing scandals of the early 2000s means he can't be rated among the true greats of the game, but I thought he was absolutely stunning.

The match itself provided a fascinating insight into the realities of playing at the top level and also the fine line between who gets the chance to put their whites on and have a go against these players. For anyone playing at the level below where they would like to play, it can be frustrating at times, especially when you have a structure in league cricket where you are able to pit your abilities against players who are easily as good as, and in some cases better than, the players strutting around the ground in their shiny colourful tracksuits.

Sussex against the 1996 Indian touring side was, from memory, live on Sky Sports and an early chance for the visitors to get ready for the first part of the international summer. For some of the local players it was an opportunity to do well on national television, giving you the chance to re watch the highlights every time you came home pissed from the pub and put the DVD on until you fell asleep.

The previous Saturday, we had played Hastings at their picturesque new ground at Horntye Park. Included in their traditionally strong side was a young off spinner called Nicky Philips who had been on the staff at Sussex for two or three years. Without being disrespectful, we thought he was a good player without thinking him so good that he was going to bowl you out just by turning up but, on this day, he was absolutely mauled by Graham Grace and Peter Mills. The more options he tried, the further they sent him and, after a few overs, he retired to the outfield to lick his wounds. Fast forward seven days and Nicky Philips had claimed the wicket of Tendulkar, one of the greatest player ever to take guard, not once but twice. He'd bagged one of the most prized scalps of all time in both innings and, for him, that was something he could tell his grandchildren, and anybody else for that matter, for the rest of his life. Was it luck, or skill, fate or fluke? I doubt Nicky would have given a toss and, quite frankly, why should he? If that had been me, I'd have got a T-shirt printed to commemorate the event.

For Keith Greenfield, the match was also one to remember as he probably played better than he ever had before. A local lad who came up through the YTS scheme, Keith was that one player on the staff who was so passionate about his team and the whole club that you hoped he would finally get the runs to warrant his breakthrough into the side. Sadly for him, it never seemed to happen often enough for him to get a regular place in the first team and, from the side lines, you never really thought he was in the same class as an Allan Wells, a Neil Lenham or even a maverick talent like Martin Speight. By 1996, the talk around the ground was that Keith had been on the staff for so long that it was time for the county to either cap him or sack him. Luckily for him his summer had started well and the match against the Indian tourists was to be arguably his finest moment. Scores of 65 and then a superb 141 not out in the second innings against Test standard opposition made people stand up and pay attention and it was not long afterwards that he was awarded his much longed-for county cap.

Watching from the cushioned chair in my office, it was hard not to feel slightly envious that someone you had regularly played against and dismissed on quite a few occasions had just taken the Indian touring side for over 200 runs in one match when you weren't sure he'd ever scored 200 runs in all the matches you'd played against him put together. On the other hand, I was pleased for him because he was a really decent bloke who had worked exceptionally hard at his game and was desperate to succeed. Were these the fine margins between luck or talent? Had they been in the right place at the right time or were they getting their rightful day in the sun after years of dedication and sacrifice? Sitting there I could think of at least ten players from the leagues who, with a change of fortune or a change of management, could have been good enough to have their picture taken for the Sunday broadsheets. I guess that's always been the case in all walks of life and, although it doesn't make it any easier, I fancy it always will be.

A few years later in the winter of 1998 we had gone back to Australia to visit friends under the premise of watching the 98/99 Ashes. Whilst staying with my old college friend Simon, we had gone out on a bender to the Crown Casino in Melbourne and upon attempting to return home in a taxi, we had picked up a ride back to where we were staying in Altona from a very pleasant Indian taxi driver. Asking whether we had been to the cricket at the MCG that day, we started nattering about things when he mentioned very patriotically that none of the players on view that day were anywhere near as great as the God that was called Sachin. Upon that rather bold statement, Simon told the nice taxi driver that I was a sort of cricketer and that I'd at one time been in the presence of the little master and even thrown a red object in his direction for him to whack it back at me. Upon hearing this amazing news, he literally stopped the car and demanded that I tell him everything about not only Sachin but also the rest of the players that I'd bowled too. He wanted to soak it all up like a sponge and asked so many questions that at times I wondered whether I was going to be taken home to meet his entire family. When the time came to leave the cab outside Simon's Melbourne home, I went to get some cash to pay the fare, only for him to refuse and tell me that anyone who had been honoured enough to bowl to Sachin Tendulkar went for free in his cab. I thought he was obviously taking the piss but he really did mean it and I guess that's just another example of trying to somehow understand just how passionate the whole Indian subcontinent is when it comes to their love of cricket.

So Sachin, if you ever do read these pages, which if I'm brutally honest I somehow doubt whether you ever will, can I take this opportunity to say that it was an absolute honour to have been in your company and thanks very much for saving me about fifty Aussie dollars when my mate had had a few too many.

25

TEST LEVEL HISSY FIT

In the middle of the field I had my hands on my waist looking like a giant double teapot while I belted out a particularly long-winded sentence, strewn with more rude words beginning with the letter F than I care to remember. Here I was, a sensible grown up, married man of nearly 30 years of age behaving like one of the spoilt children from Charlie and the Chocolate Factory. If it happened again, would I behave differently? No, probably not, your honour.

There was never much love lost between our team and the mighty Eastbourne, probably because they looked down their noses at us and thought we were crap. Sadly, they might have had a point. Historically, they had been one of the strongest sides in the county and had done well nationally as well as in the local competitions. As they always had their fair share of contracted county stars as well as the regulation gun overseas player, anything short of not getting a proper slapping when we met was a result to remember. Hang on for a boring draw and piss them off seemed to be the best we could hope for.

However, things had started to change so when we meet in early June there was only one slight difference from the year before. Whereas in the previous season the Eastbourne overseas player was a promising lad from New Zealand who was decent but nothing to have any sleepless nights about, this year's acquisition was ranked number two in the current ICC rankings with a test average above 50. Welcome back to the crease Mr Andrew Flower.

Now some might wonder why such a player would end up in the league, when you weren't actually allowed to a pay anyone for playing the game. You could pay for coaching the colts but not for anything regarding weekend cricket. He had played in the Birmingham leagues the year before where the going rate was around £15,000 for someone of his standing but I'm sure it was the attraction of doing some coaching and not paying his subs that brought him to the south coast. To be honest, there had always been plenty of clubs, including mine, who appeared to land up with players who everyone else assumed must be being paid but, for some unknown reason, were doing it for the love of the game. Players including John Snow, Imran Khan, Tong Grieg, John Edrich, Greg Richie, Tim May, Meyrick Pringle and many others had performed in the league over the years and now Andy Flower was adding his name to that long list. For some it was an outrage, making a total mockery of the league and its standing, while, in essence, they were probably just jealous that another club had had the ambition and foresight to go out and hire a big hitter to add to their ranks and improve their title chances. If he really had come for bugger all then all power to their elbow. Just as some of the names above, even if it were true, no one's believing you in the first place.

For me it was the complete opposite. I longed to challenge myself against the best and saw it as my job to try to knock them over and add their scalp to my ever-increasing list of first class and international players. The more the merrier was my attitude, and I could never understand such small-minded thinking from others, even though many came from within my own club. If you didn't want to play against such players then you should have stayed in village cricket and been a big fish in a little pond.

As Flower came out to open the innings I was desperate to prove that getting him out for bugger all the previous year was no fluke and was confident that, after a great start to the season since returning from Port Elizabeth, I could do it all over again. Despite a slight side strain, I moved in for the first ball only to see it returned at double quick speed through the covers to great cheering from the watching opposition on the boundary. To make matters worse the same fate happens twice more in the next five balls and I was right up against it. Nought for 12 of your first over is close to your worse nightmare, but it was only going to get worse.

Now it wouldn't be unfair to say that, like most fast bowlers, I could have a little moan every now and then but what happened over the course of the next ten minutes was out of character, even for me. I had definitely returned from South Africa with a lot more to say than before I left but for someone with Andy Flower's pedigree, I was going to keep very quiet and pray for the best. What I wasn't expecting was to go ape shit at my own slip cordon who, tragically for me, couldn't catch a cold that day.

Ball one of the next over caught the edge and flew straight to second slip's midriff where Pete Mills shelled the chance. Hands on head, I was distraught after the previous over and knew it could be so so costly but we all drop them and I was no different, so slowly (actually, very slowly) I walked back to my mark and waited for the next one to be hit for four because, as we all know, that's just what happens when you spill the big gun on 12. Not to be disappointed, the next one flew through gully for four runs. A loud bellowed cry came from the poor fast bowlers mouth before I had no choice other than to wander back thinking it wasn't going to be my day. That was to prove a gross understatement.

Next up, we found the outside edge again at a lovely catchable height only for this one to be left by first and second slip for each other and go for another boundary. Slightly unimpressed might have been the correct way of describing my demeanour but it didn't stop me from another huge outburst. I think the players were way too scared to come near me or say anything in fear of me throttling them on the spot. The Eastbourne players, on the other hand, saw this as probably the highlight of their season as the arrogant cock of the opposition opening bowler was having an absolute nightmare. I certainly would have.

I took it upon myself to go and field at third man for the next over as my normal fielding position at gully might have been close enough for me to kick someone in the nuts for daring to look in my direction or, even worse, trying to talk to me. My blood pressure must have been off the chart and I'm surprised I didn't burst an artery.

As I calmed myself down at the top of my mark I tried to regain my composure and told myself my luck would turn if I continued to bowl like I had in the previous over. You'll get him Stu, keep going, stay calm, you'll get him . . .

As I glided in, jumped into position and let go another decent ball in the channel outside the left hander's off stump, the world's second best ranked player duly obliged and edged the ball toward my good mate Pete Mills who was bound to redeem himself and hang on to the third straight forward chance offered up in seven balls. Of course he was. Now I really liked Pete Mills, he was a good mate, we'd been on holiday together, been to each other's weddings and would regularly go out with our wives but when I saw the small red object fall out from his hands and roll onto the ground I was, for a few seconds, all for doing a Keyser Soze on him and murdering his whole family. Nothing too drastic, just maybe his parents and immediate family, probably wouldn't have bothered with his cousins, just enough to get my point across. You know the sort of thing.

I didn't know whether to laugh or cry until some bright spark in the field tried to be a comedian and I didn't quite see the funny side. The following is apparently what came out of my mouth at a volume that the whole of the town and surrounding areas could hear.

"If you lot can't be bothered to catch the ball, then please tell me and I'll start aiming at the stumps instead. It's not like he's any good, he's only got a Test average of over 50. You've only dropped three sitters in seven balls, nothing important. I'll go back and bowl another one while you have a think about it."

Now if I was to get called to a court of law and asked to swear on the Bible, I might have to be honest and say that I might have sworn once or twice in that last paragraph but you get my drift, don't you? It's not like I want you to think any less of me as I'm happy to admit that I might have lost the plot every now and then. On that sad day in June, I was so wound up that even the umpires left me alone. In the modern days of penalty runs and suspensions I'd have probably got at least a couple of months ban.

To be fair to Andy Flower, he smiled at the end of the over and apologised, telling me he'd have probably done the same. Sadly, I only averaged about 15 in the Sussex league so it might not have been quite so costly. He was a really good bloke and we had a great chat after the match, he was complimentary about my bowling and, from such a superb player, I was very honoured. . ... once I'd calmed down about three hours later! Some bright sage or philosopher probably once said something deep and meaningful like it's only a game or that your luck will even itself out over time, and they might have a point but, in this instance and after taking into consideration their kind and wise intentions, I've decided that on days like that, they can still go and stick their thought somewhere else, thank you very much.

26

THE MAN IN THE BEIGE JACKET

When you hold your arms out and they get filled with as much free branded training gear as you can throw a stick at, that, along with the sponsored car, is a perk of the job. When you then throw in a generous visit to the tailor to have your match day clothes fitted, then that's a real bonus, especially when you get to keep them at the end of the season. Look pretty, play pretty, some will say and, in truth, I now had all the gear on and off the pitch which, when added to a 6ft 4inch frame and a proper set of fast bowling shoulders, meant I looked every inch the smartly turned out player. The only rather major problem was that I never actually got to go onto the pitch.

By mid summer, Sussex had progressed to the quarter final of the Nat West Trophy and thoughts naturally turned to the prospect of a possible return to Lord's in September and the chance to redeem themselves for losing the classic 1993 final against

Warwickshire, when it seemed to all and sundry that Sussex had scored so many runs that they only had to bowl on the cut strip to seal victory. Alas that wasn't the case as Warwickshire won off the last ball to make history and then give the BBC the chance to replay it at any given opportunity during rain breaks at their televised matches for years to come.

When the fixtures were announced, Yorkshire were to be the visitors to Hove in what promised to be a sell out and, to add to the excitement, the TV cameras would also be making a visit. Selling the hospitality packages at inflated prices was now the order of the day and it seemed that for a small county who only made a tiny profit every year in the pre Sky TV days, this was a chance to make as much money as possible while not spending too much time considering the general public who kept you afloat in the first place. In truth, as soon as the draw was made, "operation lets milk it until it turns into cheese" had begun.

With the BBC setting up the day before the match, we had the bizarre affair of witnessing a live drugs bust in the flats behind the Gilligan Stand, where someone's girlfriend had tried to flush away the merchandise before the drugs squad moved in. With sirens blazing and the meat wagons rolling in like an episode of *The Sweeney*, some drug dealer had suddenly realised that he was either going to spend an awful lot of time at Her Majesty's pleasure or end up in concrete boots either off the pier at Brighton or in a pillar at the new marina development. As he screamed his head off, I'm not sure what the men from the BBC thought of it all. This sort of thing probably didn't happen at Lord's. At one stage, it seemed that most of the staff were watching and that included the players who should have been in for a team meeting.

When match day arrived, we all had to be on parade in our smart uniforms early enough to get a parking space somewhere near the ground if one of the seven allotted parking spaces had somehow gone. There is a general impression that people change when they know that the cameras and a big crowd are around and this appeared to be the case as so many of the players drove into the ground with their sunglasses on when, in truth, it really wasn't that sunny.

While at the County Ground, I had the pleasure of working with a lovely girl called Maxine who was engaged to an ex Sussex player called Jon North. Having a county ground next door to the sea meant that the average age of the general membership was pretty old to the extent that they were sometimes describes as the coffin dodgers. Now Max could never understand how many old boys and girls we knew through the various clubs and committees and she kept making comments on the fact that she'd never met anyone who knew as many old gits as I did. On this occasion, one of the people was slightly more famous than some of the others we'd bumped into that summer.

With the ground filling up, two well-dressed gentlemen approached us as they made their way towards the Gilligan Stand, which housed the commentary boxes. David Gower and the others had already made their way up and, after resisting the chance to manhandle him and tell him how much I loved him, hard though it was, I waited for my next challenge. First, the BBC's anchorman Tony Lewis came up and was pleasant, followed by a man who I was so in awe of, I genuinely found it hard to speak which, for me, is something that doesn't happen too often. Even Maxine was stunned as, according to her, I'd barely stopped talking all season. Standing in front of me with silver hair, a serious suntan and a regulation beige jacket, was the person who had been one of the voices of my childhood. To me, Richie Benaud was the voice of summer, an absolute icon who had been made even more famous by the 12th Man tapes and by Rory Bremner to the extent he'd become, without doubt, the most famous and impersonated cricket commentator of the lot. There was only one Richie. He of the cream, the bone, the off white, the white, the ivory and the beige if you had the 12th Man CD's like we all did back in the early 90's

"Morning and, errrr, how are we all doing today?" said the great man. I'm standing gawping at Richie and he'd just said the word Morning to me. I'm seriously star struck and, to make it even better as I'm in my Sussex blazer, I think they think I look like a player or, even better, that I am one. Then the moment to top it all, the great man asks how my season's going. What shall I say? Say something quickly; it's Richie Benaud, for God's sake. Think quickly. . .ermmm, we could go with Option A "Well thanks Richie, I'm taking absolutely shit loads of wickets for East Grinstead, but not many people down here are taking a blind bit of notice so I'm still having to escort lost people to their chairs, pissheads to their over-priced hospitality suites and lost commentators to their boxes, but thanks for asking, oh and by the way, is there really any aggro between Bill and Tony on Channel 9?" or Option B "Yeah, pretty good thanks, Richie." Sadly, Option B won the day, but it was such an honour to meet the man. It also showed me, once again, that unless you play for England, have played for England or are likely to play for England sometime in the near future, no one knows what most county cricketers look like, not even the cricket commentators. We had a proper chat for a while and he came across as such an incredibly interesting and decent bloke. All I really wanted to do was take him home to meet my friends.

Sometimes meeting your heroes is a huge let down but Richie excelled himself, as I knew he would. This is the man who, when you come to think about it, probably did as much as anyone in the history of the game to make it popular and for you to want to have a go playing it. Not even WG Grace, Bradman, Warne or

Botham could claim to have had such an impact as both player and then commentator. When you sitting watching cricket on TV, everyone tries their hand at a bit of commentary and, not surprisingly, most people are crap at it because it's one of those skills that always appears to be simple – until you try it. Richie Benaud was the best and if you can come up with something like "Don't bother looking for that, let alone chasing it." And "That's gone straight into the confectionary store and out again", then you're actually a genius. To make it even better, Richie was now my new mate and that was easily good enough for me.

As the amazement stayed on my face for a while, I then had the pleasure of watching a puzzled Maxine bring me back to the real world when blurted out the line: "Stuart, who on earth were those two old duffers?" When she found out, even she was quite shocked.

As for the match, Sussex never got anywhere near enough runs for the strong Yorkshire batting line up and, by late afternoon, the ground had quietened down as the game petered out. Instead of the hoped-for exciting finish, the five o'clock flush had hit those who'd been drinking all day and they'd either fallen asleep or started to become obnoxious. Whereas at 11am the hospitality suites were places of networking and corporate speak, now some were moaning about how much it cost to watch Sussex get hammered while not everyone had enjoyed the rubbery chicken with a bit of salad on the side. Fuelled by the cheap bubbly on offer all day, a few of the clients now had enough drink inside them to fancy their chances of snaring one of the pretty young waitresses when, in reality, they had more chance of pulling off a bank robbery. It was at times like these that my varied job description needed to include the title of bouncer, as most of the stewards were in their 60s and 70s and didn't have much going for them when it came to dealing with a load of pissed up blokes who refused to leave the bars and marquees when closing time came along.

For the departing players, it was another shattered dream and, for this season at least, there wouldn't be another match on the big stage with press, television and a bumper crowd. For one or two it would be the last time they would be able to take part in such a game and they looked like they knew it. For others, it brought home the fact that they might need to look elsewhere to fulfil their ambitions. While there is the dangled carrot of possible success, the words team spirit and unity are bandied around. However, it never takes long for players to become single minded when the results go against them and then it's normally someone else's fault. The defeat to Yorkshire also brought home the fact that the season was likely to end in a drab mid table finish with what little prize money that was on offer becoming less attractive by the week.

27

I AM THE TWO DOGS MAN

In the mid-1990s Sussex were sponsored by Merrydown Cider who, in an attempt to catch the alcopop sensation sweeping the nation, tied up a deal with the Two Dogs lemonade brand from Australia. All seemed to be going well until it transpired that the owner of the brand thought he'd brought an English county cricket club rather than sponsoring the Sunday League element of the season package. I understand he was more than a little disappointed when he learnt what was actually written in the contract.

We were charged with doing something that would enhance the brand and make it visible throughout the Sunday League matches at Hove and Sussex's other grounds. With the help of a local advertising agency, we came up with the idea of putting a large hole over the dog's mouth from the company's logo and challenging fans to bowl through it from 22 or 18 yards. Surely a winner of an idea and proof that studying marketing at college all those years ago was eventually paying off. All I needed was the braces, spectacles and the over-priced suit to look the part.

We had to use a plastic ball because a real ball caused too much damage but the problem with the plastic ones was that you needed to bowl it quickly to get it to bounce high enough to get through the hole. Success meant you would become the proud owner of a Two Dogs T shirt and, because so few youngsters managed to do it, they became quite the fashion item around the south coast in 1996.

At every home match, hundreds of children would have try to win a T shirt, some having so many goes that parents would offer money for their little treasures to finally get a bloody T shirt. To make it more appealing we always let the Sussex players and the opposition have a go. Some, like Shaun Pollock, playing for Warwickshire that summer, were so desperate to get the orange ball through the big hole in the dog's mouth that he even reappeared after the mid innings break to have another go. For a bloke with more than 400 Test and 390 ODI wickets and known for his unerring accuracy, it has to be said he was a slight disappointment, though he no doubt put it all behind him by bowling Sussex out some two hours later.

Vasbert Drakes, the popular West Indian overseas player at Hove during that time, was also crap at the challenge and kept bowling the ball in on the full, which was very much against the rules. As he was on the staff and already had a T shirt, it must have been his professional pride that kept dear old Vassie coming back. In fact, he had so many goes and spent so much time there that we became big mates. He might have been a better bowler than me and he might have played in the World Cup, but he most certainly wasn't better when it came to the ultimate test of a bowler's skill.

The longer the summer went on, the more popular the Two Dogs Challenge became, to such an extent that Sussex wanted to take it on the road but that would have meant me going too which, to be honest, didn't appeal to either Mrs Simmonds or yours truly as we saw little enough of each other at that time. Less is more, I told the marketing director and, when he realised what it would cost in my time and petrol money, he quickly agreed.

Sadly, that sponsorship deal only lasted one season and so the Two Dogs challenge was consigned to history, never to be seen again. No doubt it lies covered in dust in the large dungeon underneath the offices at Hove and, like so many other things that reside there, is unlikely to see the light of day again. Like a one-season wonder with the promise of plenty more to come, it came and went but that didn't stop hundreds of kids asking me when it was going to return.

So, in 1996, Oasis were the band, Alan Shearer moved to Newcastle for a whooping world record fee of £15million, Cliff Richard unfortunately got up and sang to the crowd at Wimbledon, David Beckham was about to score a wonder goal from the half-way line and join his future wife in pop media heaven but, best of all, I was known as the Two Dogs Man by more than about 25 people, most of them spotty. Whatever did happen to the rest of them, I hear you ask.

28

CAUGHT IN THE BENEFIT TRAP

If you asked a selection of young cricketers what would consti-
tute a successful playing career, the results would be poles
apart. For some it would be getting a professional contract, others
would say making their debut for the first team, while yet others
would aim high and say that anything less than playing Test
cricket and representing your country would be a disappointment.

For many, however, the answer would be to hang around long
enough to be granted a benefit season from your county for what
approximated to ten years' service as a fully fledged first team
player. Now, in the present day, players seem to be granted a benefit for around half that, or be promised them at the end of a
contract period following a move from another club. In essence,
they were a chance to run what amounted to a small business for
one year with all profits granted tax-free by HMRC. Benefit committees were formed and organised all sorts of events, like gala

dinners, celebrity cricket matches and golf days, and made sure the begging bowls were passed around the grounds all summer long.

In the days when a player gave fantastic service to a county for at least ten years, and when they were paid not very much for six months of the year then asked to find gainful employment from October to March, the cricket-supporting public were pretty sympathetic and supportive. However, after the new Sky TV deals came into play, the average county cricketer's salary has probably tripled since the end of the 1990s and so asking Joe Public to cough up for a dinner ticket when the player is earning around £100,000 for six month's work, driving a Mercedes and then buggering off to the sun to boost his earnings by playing in a T20 tournament or two has, not surprisingly, made it slightly harder to sell these events.

The year in question was the benefit of the captain, Allan Wells, a player who had come all the way through the youth system from Sussex young cricketers to Sussex first team captain, exactly the sort of thing a benefit was designed for. Despite only playing once for England in a Test match where he was famously dismissed by Curtly Ambrose first ball after years of waiting for his chance, he was a superb batsman who, in another era, would have no doubt played far more as his talent and most importantly his weight of runs deserved. He had, however, been part of Mike Gatting's ill-fated rebel tour to South Africa in the late 1980s and so, despite missing out on his share of Test cricket, he'd been well paid for what amounted to a few weeks work and it seemed some people hadn't forgotten when it was time to donate to his benefit. Be it politics or the green-eyed monster of jealousy, some people had long memories.

As part of the running of a county, the beneficiary has to work closely with the various departments to make sure his benefit

events don't clash with the club's other affairs and that the benefactor makes the most of the opportunity without taking the piss
out of the club and the public. Most benefits are fairly similar and
formulaic but others are slightly more outside the box. One bright
ex player in the late 1970s made a fortune by holding events on
nearly every night in pubs and clubs across the county while, on
the other hand, it's not unheard of for a beneficiary to lose money
on his year's efforts. There are also stories of wives waiting for the
final cheques to be cashed before serving the divorce papers in
retaliation for too many tales of bad behaviour on away trips
over the years.

From my point of view, it was a good chance to see the work-
ings of a benefit from close quarters and to profit myself from
some of the events that were running over the summer. I played in
some golf days and made the starting line up in quite a few Sussex
XIs which gave me the chance to try and impress a few people on
the quiet. One such day was a match against my old club Lewes
Priory when I got a decent score and then bowled pretty well. The
highlight though was seeing Mr Wells himself take a quite unbelievable low, one-handed diving catch at second slip off my bowling, which still ranks as probably the best catch I've ever seen in
a game I've played in.

As there were so many functions and events throughout the
year, the downside was having to listen to the same speeches day
in, day out. No matter how funny the compare, you can only hear
some things so many times before you start hearing them in your
sleep. Alan Wells' opening line was: "Did you see Curtly Ambrose's
first ball to me in Test cricket?" which was swiftly followed by:
"No, I didn't either." It normally got a generous smattering of
laughter and, to be fair, for a beneficiary he spoke very well in
public which is more than can be said for some I have seen. Then
it was over to the very capable Roger Dakin, who doubled up as

Alan's benefit chairman and also his MC at events to make the audience laugh before trying his best to part them from their hard earned cash through various games and auction prizes. The interesting part was seeing the various business egos in the room flex their financial muscles when the bidding wars started. Some of the prices paid for a signed shirt or a framed picture of Hove, let alone a bat signed by the Sussex squad made up of at least ten players you'd probably never heard of, went through the roof once the egos had a few too many glasses of fizz and refused to be beaten by someone from a rival company across the room. It really was a case of more money than sense and, unsurprisingly, the benefactor smiled all the way to the bank.

The hard thing for the benefactor is trying to balance your playing commitments with your one chance to possibly make a life changing sum of money. You still need to perform otherwise you'll be out of the side which would cause problems regarding ticket sales to your events and threaten your deposit at various venues around the county. For Allan Wells, having to captain a side with plenty of its problems made it one extra hurdle to overcome.

29

IS THIS THE WINTER
OF OUR DISCONTENT?

Team spirit is a term that has been bandied about by sports people for years but I must admit I've never really understood it and wonder whether it actually exists. Within a group of professional sportsmen, all of whom fear failure and maybe losing their contract, it's hard to support someone else who is fighting to achieve the same things as you. From my viewpoint, I saw the damaging effect mass disharmony can create and the eventual outcome it has.

Pre-season is usually the best time to judge team unity. In the modern game, with sports psychologists, dieticians, masseurs and sides having more coaches than the company that takes them to away matches, players seem to have a lot of support when it comes to getting their head in the right place to perform. Back in 1996, though, everyone was just told to play nicely with one another, advice that was taken on board only by a few.

No matter where you work or play, office politics takes centre stage at certain times and it's no different in a professional cricket club. Everyone had an opinion on most subjects, whether they were aware of all the facts or not. From the players' point of view, everyone turned up for the first day of pre-season training hoping that this was going to be the year they made the strides they had hoped for during the winter and, for all the talk of making the first team or cementing your place through to pushing for international recognition, the moment the first team sheets were pinned up then the all-for-one-and-one-for-all sentiment vanished and the bitching and backstabbing started.

The main event of that season was when Ed Giddins, a popular figure around the club, failed a routine drugs test and, within hours, the rumours had started. For a story that was meant to be kept under wraps until all the facts were known, the whole staff knew what had happened but, if you listened to some people, you would have thought he was the head of a Columbian drug cartel not a cricketer who'd been an idiot and taken some Charlie. Like most situations, everyone had an opinion and forgot about the person in the middle. Sack him, keep him, hang him out to dry, put an understanding arm around him – all views differed to the point that even the press couldn't make their minds up once the story broke.

As the Giddins saga dragged on through the summer, the usual mutterings of player unhappiness and potential departures were never far from the surface and, once it became clear that there was absolutely no chance of any silverware, the interests of individuals came to the fore. The coach, Desmond Haynes, the legendary West Indian opener in his first year in charge, must have wondered what he'd inherited but even he wasn't immune from criticism as some players felt they needed more help from him rather than relying on his instinctive Caribbean approach. At times, he appeared so laid back that one or two didn't know if his advice was serious or not. It showed that moving from being a world-class player into the world of coaching was not as easy as it may have seemed to be at the outset. No one was immune from criticism and people were at each other's throats for various reasons.

As the season drew to a close, it became clear there was going to be a major clear-out. On hearing that he'd been banned from all cricket for 12 months for failing his drugs test, Ed Giddins was sacked by the county almost immediately. He would return with Warwickshire and go on to get his name on the honours board at Lord's, but Sussex decided they had had enough of the colourful seamer. Ian Salisbury, the England leg spinner, made no secret he was off to pastures new, Surrey as it turned out, Martin Speight went to Durham where he could take the wicket keeping gloves he so craved at Hove, and Jamie Hall, the opener, was released. His sacking seemed particularly harsh, as only a couple of seasons previously the county had blocked a move to The Oval and now, after telling him he had no future at the club, he faced the uncertainty of looking for another career. The two most surprising departures were the young all rounder Danny Law, who had just been awarded his county cap, leaving to go on a much-improved contract at Essex and then, just before Christmas, the skipper Alan Wells, amid criticism of his captaincy, signed for Kent on a lucrative five-year deal, so bringing a long and distinguished career at Hove to an end.

When it came to players speaking their mind, telling tales to whoever cared to listen, and seeing small cliques forming, it really was no different to any other sports team or organisation. If individuals don't feel they belong or think they don't have a future, then they know their time is limited and look around to see what the other options are. Some had plenty of suitors and took the chance to depart, with varying degrees of success as it turned out, while some wanted to go but the phone never rang, so they had no choice other than to stay put and repeat that well-rehearsed party line of team harmony and unity. For some it was heartfelt and honest but, for most of them, it really was complete bollocks and most people knew it.

30

GOING TO SIT RIGHT DOWN AND WRITE MYSELF A LETTER

As my summer contract was coming to an end, the prospect of spending another winter in cold old England began to loom large. Despite considering an offer of another season in Port Elizabeth, I decided that it wouldn't be fair on Jacky so, despite the obvious benefits of another summer in the sun, staying in Blighty was the only choice and I looked seriously at my options. All things were considered, from owing my own bar to emigrating to South Africa. I applied for a few cricket development officer jobs with the minor counties but missed out, with one telling me that I hadn't got the post because they were looking for someone who had finished playing and I would have been snapped up to play minor counties cricket and so would not be able to do the job I was employed to do. A bit harsh, I thought, but they might have had a point.

By early November, I decided it was time to take the bull by the horns and do what every Englishman has the ability to do – I decided to sit down and write a very stern letter. I'd seen that Jason Lewry, the left arm seamer, had been side-lined after an operation on his back and it dawned on me that, with injuries and players leaving at the end of the summer, there may not be many bowlers available for the start of the season, especially as some of the younger players would then still be up at university. Writing a letter had got me a plum job in South Africa so what's the worst that could happen if I did it again? They can only laugh and tell me to bugger off, I guess, but I was sure they'd be slightly more polite than that.

So down I sat and, in my best O level English, explained why I thought I should be given the chance to play for Sussex in the 1997 season. I listed my record in the leagues, plus my individual successes against all the Sussex players in the leagues, my performance in the county nets all summer and, of course, my exploits in South Africa where the quality of play was often of county standard. Throw in my time in the England and South Africa nets and, surely, I had a decent chance? Only the fact that I was geriatric might stand in my way. Once it was signed, sealed, given a kiss of good luck and posted, all I had to do was wait – and keep my fingers crossed.

For all the effort I'd put in over the years, Jacky and I decided I could give it another 12 months before getting what amounted to a sensible proper job – and you never knew what being able to put Sussex CCC on your CV could do for future job prospects. So wait we did but, thankfully, not for too long.

Before the reply arrived, I'd heard from at least three sources that I was in line for a chance to play for the second XI. I also found out that a few East Grinstead members had written in on my behalf, endorsing my prospects. To them, I will always be grateful, but my main supporter was Roger Dakin, Alan Wells' benefit chairman, who told the coaching staff he thought I was the best seamer in the league and that Sussex would be mad not to give me a chance and play me. Simple as that. When he phoned to tell me how the meeting went I was like a dog with two dicks.

When the letter came from second team coach Chris Waller giving me details for the winter, I felt it was vindication that I could play and I wanted to prove it. For me, it was the chance to put my money where my mouth was and finally to see if I was any good. The thing was that when I was younger, I had said that I only wanted to play a few times, to see if I could perform at that level but, as I was to find out, you need to be careful what you wish for.

31

HERE AT LAST . . .
BUT FOR HOW LONG?

With the summer fast approaching, I got some even better news than I was more than likely going to finally play some county cricket. I was going to be a father! Time to take life a bit more seriously, I thought.

The winter nets and pre-season involvement had gone well and at no point did I feel out of my depth. After the mass exodus from Hove at the end of the previous season, some new faces appeared but Sussex wasn't the place players were tearing down the motorway to join. I was being considered along with a few old faces from other counties, some promising younger players and a couple of others who, like me, were from the league and saw an opportunity.

For all the pre-season optimism, it looked like it was going to be a long, hard season on the south coast with only relative new boys Durham looking in worse shape. But I didn't give a monkey's. All I wanted to do was not get sent home and stay around long enough to play. The early move out onto grass always helped me and, on the final weekend of trials, I felt I had a good all-round weekend. Sure enough, Chris Waller confirmed I would be involved so the first part of my plan for world domination could be ticked off.

Financially speaking, I was on a similar deal to the previous year but with playing supposedly taking priority over everything else. With all the gear I looked every bit the county cricketer and, let's face it, who could tell the difference? I knew there would be people asking what on earth I was doing there and thinking their club's version of me was equally as good, if not better but I knew full well that there was so much bitching and back stabbing that went on through the club networks that unless you were about to make your test debut, there would be someone from a rival club telling all and sundry that they thought you were a hopeless imposter. I was hoping that, after all the effort and improvements I'd made, let alone a large bag of wickets season after season that I was finally in the right place at the right time.

There were some pre season friendlies against county and university sides as well as the inter club games when everyone had an early chance to impress and I felt that I was bowling well enough get through to the season without making a swift return to the coaching and marketing departments without feeling that the rug had been pulled from under my feet. I also had Roger Dakin to let me know what the coaches and captains thought with helped immensely.

With Jacky and her baby bump getting ever bigger, I finally got the call and I was off to Essex for a one dayer, followed by a three-day match at Saffron Waldron. When I arrived at Hove to travel in the new Mercedes people carrier, the other players were generally pleased to see me and wished me well. I'm not sure many of the bowlers saw me as a long-term threat – I probably wasn't – but I wasn't going to be overawed by anyone.

With a decent crowd and a good smattering of first team players on both sides, I lined up for the photographs by the Lloyds Bank-sponsored marquees and tried to look like I belonged. I had the same shirt as all the others, with the Sussex crest on and so that was a start. When the call finally came to get ready, I prayed to at least land the first ball somewhere near the cut strip and improve from there. That I did and, with Essex nicely poised only two wickets down and looking to push on towards a good score, I managed to get Stephen Peters to top edge one to the keeper and there it was, my name in the wickets column for all time. Small things, I know, but it meant absolutely masses to me. Thankfully it was to get better and I bowled my ten overs straight to finish with three for 35 and, with a couple of dropped chances, it could have been better. Captain Neil Lenham was full of praise and I finished off talking a couple of good high catches on the boundary to put everything in the "pretty good start" bracket.

As I sat in the dressing room and enjoyed the plaudits of a job well done, I sensed that the previous good wishes from a couple of bowlers were being replaced by unkinder thoughts as now, if I carried on doing what I'd just done, my chance to jump ahead of them in the all important next cab off the rank might be heading my way. That is, in essence, the cut-throat nature of professional sport. Someone is always looking to take your spot, no matter how left field their selection may have been at the start.

During the break, I chatted with a couple of lads I knew from the leagues and thought that, if things went well, I could be in with a shout of the man of the match award. However, as Raj Rao scored a superb hundred to see us to victory, he got the whopping great bottle of champagne, although I did get a mention in the speeches and a nice round of applause. Touching, but still no champers.

Back at the hotel, things had all changed. Almost half of the one-day side went off to play in a championship match at Hove and some more trialists came in for the three-day game. The marquees came down, the chairs went away and what you were left with was a fairly soulless, empty ground with 22 players who all wanted to be playing somewhere better. As he left for the drive back to Hove, Neil Lenham told me that if I bowled like that again, then you never know what could happen in the future. Sadly, that was as close as I'd ever get to the first team. To make matters worse, I was being hampered by a pain in my left calf just when I needed to be making the most of a great first impression.

Cheap hotels and sharing a room with a bloke who snored and kept changing his voicemail to make it sound like he was a full time pro instead of a match money player was not a great experience but if someone had told me that, after bowling like I had the previous day I'd only bowl seven overs in two innings of the three day match, I would not have believed them. But, with a different captain, I barely got a chance and watched as his team mates from Eastbourne dominated, so much so that a huge row kicked off in the changing room over his bowling changes – or lack of them. I sat there quietly in the corner and listened as the bitching went into overdrive and the frustrations of a few weeks now began to come out in public. In hindsight, I should have pulled up injured and gone home after the one-day match, but I was keen to impress. I didn't but you can't always get it right. Battling through injury had always been a strength but, in this instance, it had done me no favours at all.

To be honest, I've often sat down and wondered what might have happened if even one of those dropped catches had stuck and I'd have ended up with a match winning performance on debut rather than a decent first attempt. Still, after all the years of finally waiting to fulfil my dream, I have to say I was thrilled to get home.

32

PLEASE SIR, CAN I HAVE ANOTHER GO PLEASE SIR?

When I look back on that first match for Sussex, an event I'd looked forward to for so long, one thing always sticks in my mind. When I knocked the stump out of the ground for my third wicket, I turned in celebration but all I saw were coaches and injured players on the boundary reading the paper, not even noticing what I'd done. Slightly unimpressed, to say the least, it did make me wonder how many of us were there just to make up the numbers while the coaches waited for the players they really did rate to become available.

Being injured and desperate to play is a hard combination to deal with and it was something that seemed to happen to me at the wrong time. While I was out injured, I was back at Hove for the other part of my employment and watched as a strong Surrey side destroyed my team mates from the previous week, making me appear a much better player by simply not playing.

When I returned, I bowled Horsham out and then, the following week, took my best-ever league figures of 9-51, only missing out on the elusive ten by getting the only player I didn't dismiss out off a no ball. It was only when I'd got the seventh wicket that I realised what might have been. I'd never bowled quicker. The ball was flying out of my hand and most of the 51 runs came from edges. It was one of those days that you dream about, when everything clicks into gear.

As it happened there were to be no more call ups and no more chances to live out your dreams and any hopes that you could push for a late chance at a career that you'd always dreamed off had been extinguished. I was too old to try my luck at another county when in reality I should have been doing this sort of thing when I was much younger instead of kicking a football around with my mates. Still I'd played some pre season and championship matches for Sussex with reasonable success including bowling a young Marcus Trescothick second ball of the match, and seeing the huge potential of Glamorgan's Simon Jones. Surrey's Alex Tudor also impressed and really hit the bat hard and you wonder why he didn't have a better career. However, sometimes I do look back and wish that I'd aimed higher than just playing a few matches and actually been able to pull off the improbable.

By mid-summer, I knew the inevitable call was coming and, sure enough, Chris Waller phoned to tell me that it was unlikely that I'd be picked again as the university staff players were returning and the club had to look to the future. He kindly thanked me for my efforts and hoped I'd enjoyed the matches I'd played. I appreciated the call. It was all very amiable but the moment I hung up, I'm not ashamed to say I cried my eyes out. I knew it was a huge long shot but the calf problem and my age had not exactly helped my long-term prospects. When I saw Peter Moores at Hove, he said that the county just couldn't sanction an untried

30-year-old, no matter how well I'd done. Not a huge surprise but still hard to swallow.

With the months ticking down until the birth of our first child and with me still busy at Hove, there was a mixture of excitement and agony as I had to watch match after match thinking I could be playing, but that was the downside of a job where everything you wanted was placed in front of you – you just weren't able to grab it and have a go.

My club season also suffered from the "after the Lord Mayor's Show" side effects and it petered out to the extent that I even thought of missing a couple of games. Thankfully, things improved when I was offered the chance to go and pro in Cape Town. Jacky was keen to have her maternity leave in the sun and a chance to combine that with me playing and coaching cricket seemed the perfect arrangement. We weren't actually sure what having a small child would entail, but we were sure we could do it.

After speaking to Dave Emslie about the prospect of returning to Port Elizabeth, he was honest enough to admit that the province was so financially strapped that they couldn't afford anyone from overseas, even though he would have loved me to return. What he did do though was contact Paul Phillipson, the former Sussex player who now worked at Western Province Cricket, and gave me a glowing reference. Calls were made and, soon afterwards, a job offer arrived from Cape Town Cricket Club for the 1997/98 season as their player/coach. A decent salary, Mercedes to drive and a healthy win bonus all presented themselves on the paper ready for me to sign on the dotted line. All we had to do was have a baby on time, move into my parents' house while we rented out ours, sort the cat out for six months and then get on the plane so we could see the pretty mountain for six months.

What could possible go wrong? As it turned out, plenty. . .

33

WAITING AND WAITING AS THE NATION MOURNS

With a baby bump the size of the mountain we were about to go and visit, we sat patiently waiting for child number one to appear and, as such, the weeks past with a mixture of pure excitement and utter trepidation. However, the events of August 31, 1997 were to change everything.

When the news filtered through about the death of Princess Diana, it sent the media into overdrive and, royalist or not, you had no choice other than to be taken in by the tragic events in that Paris tunnel. State funeral, days of sombre music and millions of people lining up to sign the books of condolence were just some of the things that happened when the country and its people went into a mini meltdown.

On a smaller – and obviously less important – scale, it had an impact on cricket in Sussex as the funeral coincided with the last Saturday of the league season, which, that year saw at least three sides still in with a chance of winning the title. At the start of the week, several club members began complaining that the first and second teams were planning to play on the day of the funeral and it soon caused a major rift at the club. It quickly became obvious we were not the only club in this situation and things changed again when, in light of complaints from county members, Sussex withdrew all their players from the league on that weekend. The local newspaper, The Argus, then reported that they had been contacted by a group who were threatening to dig up the wickets of every club intending to play that Saturday and so, for the first time in its history, the Sussex League postponed all its fixtures until the following weekend.

This delay meant that, as most overseas players return home a couple of days after the final weekend, clubs would have to do without their hired guns for the final push. Not that this meant anything to us as we'd enjoyed the services of a young Aussie leg-spinning all-rounder who had averaged fewer than ten with the bat and actually managed not to take a single wicket with the ball all season. For a country that was dominating world cricket, it was our bad luck to pick up the only Australian cricketer in the world who was unbelievably hopeless.

Diana's funeral also affected businesses in town where a friend had to close his clothes shop after threats to throw bricks through his windows if he opened. So a man who made sure he kept his shop open and manned on the day of his own mother's funeral, had to shut it for a woman he'd never met and didn't particularly like. All very bizarre.

So, as the country watched the funeral from start to finish, you couldn't help but think it was nothing other than incredibly sad that the most photographed and followed woman in the world was no longer with us. You also had to admire how the establishment had managed to put on such a ceremony in such a short time. It was said on the news that the minute's silence was observed beautifully across the entire country that day, all except at one house in De La Warr Road, East Grinstead where Jacky's mum somehow managed to talk through the entire ceremony. The only surprise was that Jacky didn't go into labour half way through Elton John's new version of *Candle in the Wind*.

The following weekend turned into something of a massive anti climax as many sides were completely ruined by absences and drop outs and, as we were playing potential champions Bexhill, this was somewhat embarrassing as the side we put out would barely have given an U13 side much of a game. Sure enough we were hammered out of sight as the bottles were uncorked and the new champions celebrated long into the night. I had spent the day with a borrowed mobile phone on standby in the scorebox with my car pointed in the direction of the hospital but didn't get the call. After that, we waited and waited until, finally on September 23, 1997 and after a couple of false alarms, Hannah Louise Simmonds appeared. I was the proud new owner of a beautiful baby daughter and life, as I knew it would never be the same again. Vicious rumours that her middle name was after the pop star Louise are still, even today, being neither confirmed nor denied. With this new sense of responsibility being taken seriously, surely going to the other side of the world to bowl red balls at three sticks wasn't in any chapter of the Good Parents' Guide?

The move out of our house was well underway when Hannah arrived and, for several days, I moved boxes over to my parents ready for the flight to Cape Town. One of the last things I had to do was to get Cynthia the cat her annual injections as the tenants had agreed to look after her for the six months. Taking her to the vet was always a bit of a struggle as the sight of her cat basket normally meant she buggered off under the stairs for a day or two but this time I'd managed to mentally defeat the moggy and had her imprisoned in the wicker contraption long enough to have her sitting comfortably in the waiting room when our name was called. I went into the clinic only to find, standing in front of me, the Australian captain of local rivals Three Bridges with a massive cat-shaped syringe in his hand. We might have exchanged pleasantries a few times, and I might have given him a pretty big send off a few weeks earlier when I'd got him out, but I didn't expect him to go to all the trouble of dressing up as a vet so he could take his revenge out on my cat. I looked helpless as I thought he was going to give Cynthia a lethal injection and would be lying if the words "Shit, he's going to kill the cat" hadn't crossed my mind. Thankfully, Mr Dave Butchart was a much better bloke out of his whites and, not only did he not kill Cynthia, he did the job for nothing and wished me all the best for my next foreign assignment. Like all good Aussies, what's said on the field, stays on the field.

The time had finally come to say our farewells, board the plane and depart for what would be my final overseas assignment. The very pretty mountain would be in view in around 11 hours' time and then the fun would start.

34

WRONG TERMINAL, WRONG CLUB

I probably should have seen the writing on the wall long before I stepped onto the pitch for my new club. On the face of it, things looked promising. I had a decent basic salary, Mercedes for the summer and was at a club with a swimming pool in its complex who were in need of a bowler and with a keen young side to coach. In reality, I should have checked the small print on my contract because what I walked into bore no relation to what was offered on the original letter.

When the challenges of travelling with a three-week-old child to another continent finally hit you, it's probably too late to go back but we managed it well and, with our first experience of a child cot on the plane not proving too testing, we arrived at Cape Town International ready to be picked up by the Cape Town Cricket Club chairman Terry Wallace. The only problem was that he was nowhere to be seen and only turned up when he realised we hadn't gone to the domestic terminal. Pleasantries over, on the journey to where we were staying in Rondesbosch I asked who we were playing the following Saturday. The pause was definitely longer than it should have been, and he looked pretty sheepish as he told me I was going to start the season in the second team. He could have asked me to open the car door and jump out onto the highway and I would have been less shocked. The explanation was poor and it was the first in a day of ringing alarm bells.

One bright light in the gloom was meeting our new landlords, Shirley and Sandy Rossiter, who lived in a lovely house in Muir Road and had done out their annex for the rental market. We immediately hit it off and the fact that we had a cute baby certainly did us no harm. That evening we were invited for dinner and have stayed firm friends ever since. Before then I had been picked up by Terry Wallace again and taken off to meet my new team mates and officials at CTCC. Although the ground looked impressive, you soon realised that nothing actually worked. The wicket had a disease so there was to be no cricket on the square for a fortnight, the swimming pool was the size of a stamp and, unless green pools were all the rage in 1997, then I suspected it needed a bloody good clean. However, the main problems were caused by the people who ran the club and, more importantly, by the pictures hanging on the walls in the pavilion.

When I had agreed to come to CTCC, the captain had convinced the committee that what they needed was a seamer and he had managed to get his way. We'd spoken on the phone several times prior to my departure and I liked the sound of what he was trying to achieve. However, as I was told within an hour of my arrival, the vote to invite me over had been very close and the real problem was that the captain had now moved to Durban on business for two years. The one person who really wanted me in the team was no longer part of the setup and so, less than three hours after our plane had touched down, there was no doubt I was up shit creek without a paddle.

Unbelievably, worse was to come. As I had a beer with the new skipper, a thick set man by the name of Eric Halverson, he thought it polite to inform me that, in his view, overseas players should be banned in order to allow local players to learn to play at that level. When I told him we would never play an overseas player in the second team back in the UK, he told me that he didn't care what happened in England and that he didn't rate county cricket, or anything English for that matter. I now appear to be going down shit creek blindfolded.

The photographs on the clubhouse walls told a lot of the story, the main problem being what the club had done during isolation. The pictures showed the hugely strong sides CTCC had been able to put out week in, week out during the late Seventies and Eighties. The bowling attack was essentially the national side's opening attack of Garth Le Roux and Stephen Jefferies added to Robin Jackman and the overseas player was England's Paul Jarvis. Ken McEwan and several provincial players made up the batting line up and they were so strong that Les Ryan, who I'd come across playing at Hastings and was a superb bowler, played most of his time in the CTCC second team. So strong and so dominant had they been that the long sock brigade on the committee thought that current club cricket was disgraceful by comparison.

The whole experience was a real punch to the guts and I went home incredibly deflated but fresh in the knowledge that at least I would be driving around Cape Town in a nice Mercedes. To cap the day off just perfectly, I was presented the keys to a 1979 version that looked like the sort of car Arthur Daley would have tried to flog to you without any success. It drank as much oil as it did petrol and ended up costing me a fortune while making me look like a poor man's drug dealer. The following day I went to the Western Province offices to meet Paul Phillipson who had arranged my deal with CTCC and he seemed genuinely distressed by what I told him. Although I would do plenty of coaching for him and bowled regularly at the nets at Newlands, he was fairly powerless to help me too much and was seriously pissed off with how things had panned out.

The final port of call regarding work was at S.A. College High School (SACS) where I worked every afternoon for Chris Fletcher who introduced me to the other coaches helping with the sessions. When I told them where I was playing, I was greeted with either "God, good luck" or "Poor you". One even asked whether I was this year's sacrificial offering. It seemed recent history suggested that the overseas player had been messed around year after year and the same would most likely happen to me. All I could do was perform to the best of my ability and hope I could win the doubters overs. My first match was away at Tech Mutual which was played over two weekends, as in Port Elizabeth. By the end of day one we'd batted and I'd made a decent effort to be not out and then grabbed the two wickets that fell by the evening so, personally, I was pleased with my day's work. The general chat among the second teamers was that, unless I became Allan Donald, then I'd be up against it. The following Saturday I came back to bowl Techs out and finish with figures of six for 20 and, even though we collapsed in our second innings to lose badly, I again finished unbeaten. Surely I'd done enough to prove my worth and ability and make the selection for the next match, especially as the first team had been hammered out of sight at Bellville.

Bizarrely, when I arrived at training, I was called in to be a witness as one of the second team players had a gripe at the selection panel for dropping him to the third team and it was only then that I realised that I hadn't been picked for the next match against UCT. I was shattered and truly realised what I was up against. It was like trying to win an argument when nobody was prepared to listen to the facts. It was a fight that would continue for the whole of my stay at CTCC and one that I was never going to win.

35

WEEKENDS WITH
MR GIBBS AND MR KALLIS

With my chances of a successful season in the shadow of Table Mountain looking fairly grim, I tried to maintain my dignity when plenty around me seemed to take great pleasure in my struggles. I've always wondered whether some of the local players took quiet delight in seeing someone from another part of the world falter, as it re-affirmed their view that the standard of cricket they played here was higher than elsewhere. As the weeks went by, the more gossip worthy I became and there seemed to be two distinct camps where you could park your opinions. The first was that I was the latest in a long list of players who'd been sawn off at the knees and that I'd been given no chance to prove myself, even though my CV and references were impressive and that I'd done very well in the Eastern Province A league. The second line of thought was that I was English and therefore, by simple definition I was useless and the quicker I was back on the plane to Heathrow, the better.

My major mistake was playing in that opening match which meant I was ineligible to play for any other team that season. As mistakes go, it was turning out to be a bit of a whopper. I'd forgone the chance to tell CTCC where they could stick their plum overseas gig and was now left with no chance other than to play where they picked me as my newly-found fatherly responsibilities meant I still needed that monthly pay cheque. As I prepared for the second week of fixtures in the second team I received an early call from the chairman of selectors to inform me that one of the players was ill and I was to make my first team debut against the traditionally strong UCT side. When I told him that I had no idea how to get to the university grounds, he told me that wasn't his problem and suggested I left early in case I got lost. Not so much as a good luck which, as the season went on, didn't surprise me at all.

Finding the ground was, indeed, tricky but when I eventually pitched up I got the distinct feeling that most of my team-mates would have preferred me not to be there. The side was full of players who had all had the chance to play some form of professional cricket around the world and, if that came as an advantage in terms of experience, it also meant there were some very bitter players who still simmered about their lack of fortune and moaned about current players who they thought should be their team-mates. Different countries, similar issues.

As the dressing room waited to hear the result of the toss, the subject turned to UCT's overseas player Nick Preston who had just left Kent and was intending to settle full time in Cape Town where he'd been wintering for several years. Nick was one of the coaches at SACS who'd been less than enthusiastic about CTCC's treatment of players over the years and we'd hit it off while working together during the week. One of my new team-mates did say something along the lines of him being "nowhere near good enough to play first class cricket", words that came back to haunt him when Nick returned figures of six for virtually nothing as we were bowled out for around 150, which looked woefully short of a decent total.

Personally I did well, taking three for around 30 and, but for a couple of chances, could have had more as we restricted UCT to around 100 for six at the end of the first day's play. I was thrilled that, by being the pick of the bowlers, I'd probably got a bit of a monkey off my back and won over a hard crowd. You can think again on that one, Stuart, as it turned out. Between the two Englishmen, we'd taken nine of the 16 wickets that fell that day as we'd simply bowled an English type length and got the rewards we'd deserved but not too many people wanted to acknowledge that fact.

When I returned for the second weekend, I didn't even get to bowl again as UCT racked up a big first innings lead then Nick Preston picked up another five wickets to help his side to an innings victory. The huge egos in the dressing room didn't see this as much of a problem as they all seemed to fall into the "class is permanent" school of thinking to explain three defeats from three matches. For a salary that would definitely benefit from some win bonuses, it seemed that fallow times lay ahead.

The only benefit was that I was sure I'd done enough to get into the next match against Green Point who included Brett Schultz, now playing his provincial at Western Province and making a comeback from another injury, ready to terrorise the clubbies standing in his way. For me in my current situation, he was possibly the last person in the world I wanted to see and when my time came to face the music, this time it only took a few balls from the left armer to leave me with only two stumps and the lonely walk back to join my team-mates, many of whom had fallen in a similar manner.

It seemed that every team had the potential to select an array of top class cricketers all ready to eat you up and spit you out and it often depended on whether there was a provincial match which would involve the pros, leaving mere club players to play at our level. When we played Constantia, their week one side consisted of internationals Gary Kirsten and a young Jacques Kallis, provincial players Alan Dawson, Sven Koenig and the extremely rapid Dean Paine plus the Hampshire overseas player John Stephenson which was as strong as most county sides in England. However, on the second weekend once the tourists had flown to Pakistan and Western Province had a match in Durban, only Stephenson remained. Although Kallis made only 20-odd before chopping the off spinner onto his stumps, it was his bowling that really surprised me as he was far, far quicker than he looked on the television. He was genuinely quick, his first ball thudding into my batting gloves quicker than I could say "Good Lord that's fast." In the following weeks, he would score his first Test century in Melbourne and the legend was being formed. It's a strange feeling knowing that I was on the same pitch in a competitive match as Kallis, someone who would go on to become one of the greatest players ever to grace the sport.

However, of all the players I came across that winter, no one came near to being in the same league as a young Herschelle Gibbs. If my memory's correct, he'd already played a couple of Tests and a handful of one-day internationals but was nowhere near the player he would become. Playing for a side not really fancied by the much more lofty players from CTCC in a 45 over per side cup match, the only blessing for me was that I was injured and therefore didn't have to suffer at the hands and blade of someone playing at a different level than the rest of us. I'll make no excuses and say that, at that stage of the season, I might as well not have been selected anyway, such was my lack of respect for some at the club, but it was still an absolute pleasure to witness the Gibbs onslaught. With the reputation of being a bit of a playboy – an image he had reinforced by turning up in a flashy Golf GTI with a couple of ladies who were extremely easy on the eye – he went on to put on a batting display of such skill that it simply was a thing of beauty to behold. At one stage, he went down on one knee and hit a flat six over extra cover that flew out of the ground only to be stopped on the full by a large wall. It was one of many audacious strokes that most other players simply wouldn't dream of playing. The CTCC attack were simply cannon fodder as Gibbs strode his way to a massive hundred and in the process he steered his team to a huge win. I'd never ever seen a clean hitting display like it. In fact, I'd never seen anything like it before or since that day. Some people are blessed from above and Mr Gibbs was certainly one of them.

36

HARSH LESSONS
AND EARLY EXITS

A wise man once told me that, no matter how bad things might appear to be, the sun will always rise in the morning, and hope will return. Generally, I could see where he was coming from but, at this time, each new day seemed to bring the same shit that had been churned out the day before. I just thought I was in the wrong place at the wrong time and quite often wondered why I bothered to pitch up in the first place. Would anyone have missed me.

The season was nearing the half way mark and we were play-ing out in Kuils River, a township near Cape Town. They had been granted A league status with the promise of no relegation for five years in an attempt to promote cricket in the area and give a focus to the young talented players trying to make their way towards the professional game. Not surprisingly, the facilities weren't of the highest standard but, as a side, they were competitive and had some outstanding players, so it was always likely to be a tough assignment. What I didn't expect was for what appeared to be the whole population of the township to descend on the ground during the afternoon and take great pleasure in abusing the visiting Englishman.

I was well aware that a few of the senior players didn't want me at the club and they had made it quite clear what they thought of overseas players but, when the crowd started arriving in great numbers and parking themselves on the boundary's edge, it didn't take a genius to work out who was going to be posted down at fine leg after his marathon spell of three opening overs had finished. The large majority of the crowd were off their faces and becoming more vocal and abusive as they consumed more and more drink. This will only last for a few overs, I thought, but then, in something akin to Tom Brown's schooldays, the captain decided to push mid off back onto the boundary, meaning that I was there again for every ball of every over, something several in the side thought hilarious. Now this might have seemed amusing for a few overs but it was becoming a real nightmare for me as the abuse levels rose and I feared someone might actually turn on me. A couple of the players offered to swap but they were sent packing and so there I stayed until the end of play. In all my years playing the game, I'd never felt so humiliated.

I returned home that night, sunburnt and mentally beaten to a pulp, knowing that, despite trying my hardest, I was fighting an unwinnable war. The standard line of the team needing to play an extra batter was pulled out for the first round of matches after the break and, in all honesty, it was a relief. So, for the second half of the season I played knowing full well that even if I got more wickets than I could throw a stick at, I was probably the last person was going to get selected. I decided I'd use my remaining matches to learn how to bowl a decent slower ball – successfully, as it turned out – and when the time came for Jacky and Hannah to return, I arranged an early exit in March and travelled home with them.

I can always remember looking out of the plane window at Cape Town International and wondering where and why it all went so badly wrong. Sometimes the mountains and scenery dulled the fact that things hadn't worked out but, as the season wore on, I can't ever remember having less confidence. When I returned from PE, I felt like a proper player who could take on anyone, anywhere but now, two years later, I felt like a complete failure and had been found out as the imposter I surely was. Still, when I looked over at the chubby, bald headed little girl in her baby grow with a massive smile, I did realise there were more important things in my life.

Despite all the disappointments of the previous six months, in a strange way I'd learnt an awful lot, which would help in the years ahead. For me, Cape Town is simply the most beautiful place I've ever seen and, almost 20 years later, that opinion has not changed. You could offer me anywhere else in the world and, although it might be nice, it still wouldn't be a patch on Cape Town. We made lifelong friends, spent an incredible time with Hannah and, even on the cricketing side, I'd played against some world class players, worked and coached at some brilliant places with some terrific children and, thanks to Paul Phillipson, played at Newlands under lights; an incredible experience. So, despite the nightmare of CTCC, it hadn't been all-bad. I guess that, as we now have a second home in Camps Bay and get out to Cape Town as much as we can, means that wise old sage knew what he was talking about. Maybe the sun does always come up over the mountain every morning and, thankfully, I've been there to see it do just that many, many times since.

37

CAPE TOWN HANGOVER

The funny thing about confidence is that it never seems to be much of an issue until you're prepared to admit that you're in the shittiest form of your life and there doesn't seem to be anything you can do about it. Then, as all good pundits will tell you, you're suffering from a massive fall in confidence, which is not exactly PHD level analysis, but it nearly always seems to be the standard answer to any player's problem.

Now if you'd had the pleasure of seeing me try to perform in the early days of the 1998 season, you've have thought that I'd never bowled a cricket ball in my life. I'd be the first to admit that, on returning from Cape Town, I was struggling to understand how things had gone so badly and would admit that my cricketing mojo was at an all-time low. I thought that, being back home and among people I knew, everything would sort itself out but, in reality, I was starting to think maybe I was useless and I'd finally been found out. Sadly, the first two matches did nothing to change things and, even though I came up with the usual excuses of pre-season rustiness or exhaustion caused by playing in South Africa, I couldn't help but fear I might be something of a busted flush.

Despite interest from other clubs, I'd remained loyal to EGCC and, with the added extra of a new coaching role to help me financially; I felt that I needed to perform on the pitch. After the second dreadful performance in the early rounds of the National Knockout, where I bowled so slowly that I would barely have taken the bails off, I realised I looked like a poor player and wondered whether some of the old bastards at CTCC were right all along. However, like all nice stories, this tale had a happy ending.

With the season starting properly at Brighton against a side full of Sussex pros, you knew you'd be in for a tough ride which was exactly why I'd chosen to play at this level. With the second ball of the innings, Sussex's Rajesh Rao edged me to second slip and it was as if someone had instantly jumped off my shoulders and all the frustrations of the previous six months vanished into thin air. I still deserved my place among the best players and my relief was palpable. I finished the game with four wickets and repeated that the following week against an equally strong Chichester side where I bowled one of the quickest spells I can remember. Within the space of a few weeks I'd gone from the depths of bowling hell and returned as someone who was absolutely flying and that, I suppose, must come down to believing in myself. I felt I belonged and that I was back in a team which relied heavily on my performances and who knew 100 per cent that I could play. If that all fitted nicely into the all-consuming confidence box, then I was more than happy to pay the shrink and get back to work.

Now 1998 was the year when the ECB decided to introduce Premier Leagues and we knew that, at the end of the season, the league would be split into two with the lower teams splitting from the big guns. So, unless they drew them in a cup competition, a team like Sidley would quite conceivably never play against a team like Horsham again. Still, strength versus strength seemed the way to go. For a side like us, we needed to get off to a good start to make sure we ended up in the top ten for the following season and that is what happened, winning three and drawing one of our first four matches meaning we were second in the table with what looked like the best team we'd had in years.

Our good start, however, was about to be knocked for six. Before the season began, I'd arranged to bring a young cricketer from the youth set up at Western Province called Allahudien Palaker over to England. Quickly known as Pally, because no one could pronounce his first name, he was a batsman who bowled more than handy off spinner and he joined a long list of players who had come from the republic to play for East Grinstead. However, it became clear the club had made a clerical error and not filled in his registration forms properly and so we were set to start the fifth round of matches with zero points. Despite much sympathy and a heated EGM, the penalty stood and, despite being one of the best sides in the league, we were well and truly in the shit.

I'd been in the form of my life, getting a hatful of wickets and even scoring some valuable runs down at No 8. I was delighted to be getting a reputation for knocking over many of the Sussex pros and overseas players yet, when it came to Monday mornings, I'd be heading off to another set of schools while the blokes I'd turned over at the weekend would be heading off for another round of county cricket. As annoying as it was, I was getting accustomed to doing it without blinking. One slight pick-me-up was that I'd been selected in the newly formed Sussex Board XI, which was made up of pros, prospective young cricketers and the best club players in the county. It also came with the carrot of a place in the early stages of the following year's Nat West Trophy, something I did not want to miss out on. Thankfully, the wickets kept coming and so my prospects of making the final XI appeared quite positive.

With our point's deduction, we needed to do very well in our final matches to make the cut for the following season's Premier League. We delivered in some style and went into our last match of the season against Bexhill needing a win to make the top ten. As would only happen in England, with the game evenly poised at the halfway stage, the heavens opened, leaving us with a serious run chase to get home. What followed would not have looked out of place in a classic British farce. As the rains eventually ceased, we tried between us to get the covers off. Half the side pulled one way, half the side pulled the other and – disaster! – All the standing water on the sheeting poured right down the middle of the cut strip and, with that soaking, we watching our efforts literally go down the drain. It also meant that, despite a season that would have normally seen us finish around fifth, we had to face up to life in Division Two which, for some of the players we had at the time, was absolutely criminal.

As the cricket season came to a close and, as a family we prepared for our first full winter at home for a while, I had to wrestle with a generous offer from Northerns Goodwood, Pally's club back in Cape Town, who, with Mr Palaker Snr as their chairman, had made a big effort to get me back as their player/coach and, despite my best-ever season and the fact that I was still desperate to prove I could be a success in the WP A league, I had to reluctantly turn it down as, with a growing family and a new business venture, I needed to take my big boy pills and start to behave like a proper grown up for once. It was, in effect, the end of my time as an overseas player and, even though I was enjoying family live and looking forward to what lay ahead, I'd be lying if said I wasn't upset at the idea of never being able to do it again.

The shake-up in the league had started the first real free-for-all when it came to poaching and recruiting players, who now had to think about the standard they played at and which clubs could match their ambitions. Many sides, including ours, saw some of their best players move on to play in the new Premier League and attempts to play the loyalty card to keep players were not particularly successful. For me, I'd taken more than 60 wickets in all first team league and cup matches at under 10 a piece and yet, despite being in the prime of my fast bowling life, I was being asked to forgo my ambitions and many generous offers to stay at a weakened club to try and win promotion the following year. It would also be the first time I'd get to see how the loyalty game really worked out for all parties.

38

WITH HINDSIGHT, PROBABLY NOT MY BEST EVER DECISION

There are certain things that people will try to teach you when you're young, many of them in the hope that you'll learn enough not to come to any physical or emotional harm or, worse, still make a complete tit of yourself or lose a boatload of money. Look both ways when you cross the road, never talk to strangers, don't put your fingers in the plug socket, don't ever eat the yellow snow and never reply if a random African prince tells you he wants to put a large sum of money into your bank account for a few days. All sensible advice at various stages of your life it has to be said, but one thing that no one ever tells you is that opening a specialist cricket shop is a truly dreadful idea and you'd have actually been better off buying some magic beans at the market. At least you'd have been able to climb up the beanstalk to see what was there instead of contemplating throwing yourself from the top of it when the VAT bill needed paying and you were potless.

Like most great ideas, it had started promisingly enough towards the end of the Cape Town season and seemed like a perfectly hatched plan that would fit nicely alongside playing and coaching as well as giving flexibility to the ever-growing Simmonds clan. Research was duly done, I knew about the product, understood who was likely to purchase it and, as I knew a lot of people in cricket and others who ran sport at schools, it seemed like a sensible plan. Maybe one that wasn't destined for world domination but certainly one that had the potential to grow into a successful business meaning that the mortgage and child care could be handled slightly more easily.

On my return to the UK, I began by selling Newbery products, which was a good start. I wanted to expand and sell more than one brand but what I never really wanted was the expense of having an actual shop. I soon realised that cricket manufacturers were actually run like small cottage industries, many struggling to survive, selling out of large containers with a desk and a computer in the corner and unable to pay for more than a couple of staff. They were all desperate for business and, once you had their products, they didn't seem to care how you went about selling it. Gray Nicolls and Slazenger both insisted that you had shop premises and, as they were the two biggest companies in the cricket market, you needed to have them on your advertising posters if you wanted to be taken seriously.

As the cricket season came to a close and the revenue from selling cricket products understandably fell, I decided, to help us through the winter, it would be sensible to add hockey to the company name and thus Two Season Sports was born. In fact, hockey proved far more profitable as, despite being a good game, it is a minor sport and regular sports shop never stocked anything other than a £25 Grays stick and some shin pads. If cricket was poorly catered for on the high street, then the provision for hockey was laughable. Getting the best hockey brands wasn't hard – again only Grays refused to sell to us – but we had enough to offer and mobile shops at clubs and tournaments proved a profitable exercise.

The best thing about hockey was that you did not need to hold a lot of stock and there were only so many things you needed to play the game. With cricket, there were hundreds of different sizes of protection bags and different types of shoes and, of course, when you added in the sodding left handers and the stock they needed, then ordering became an expensive operation. Even off the field, left handers were now causing me grief!

With hindsight, as the garage got fuller, I should have stayed and just got a bigger garage, but I decided to take the plunge, went to the bank manager and signed my life away in order to raise enough money to take premises on the basis that, with more footfall and somewhere to hang the stuff up properly, I might actually look like I knew what I was doing. Even Grays and Gray Nicolls eventually ended up in the brochures even though I was none too keen on them after they'd refused to do business with me before. What I didn't have, though, was enough knowledge of the retail industry and the complexities that came with it. I made the classic mistake of over ordering, thinking that what I liked, everyone else would too and, looking back at my early business plans and projections, it wouldn't have been unfair to suggest that they had been filled in by a young child with a whole bunch of coloured pencils.

What I did have, though, was an excellent online presence that was provided by my brother Paul, who was a complete star and spent hours building me a superb new website that, for a while, proved very successful and dovetailed nicely with the retail prem-ises. There were big signs outside and we looked like a proper business, adding brands like Oakley to the company. To thank him for all his sterling work, I gave Paul a 10 per cent share in the business but, as the years wore on and the banks and tax man started taking more than their fair share of what little I had left, I could have given him 100 per cent of everything because, as everyone knows, 100 per cent of nothing is, sadly, still nothing. The only upside of the whole affair seemed to be that I was never short of a decent pair of sunglasses.

39

STAR SPANGLED THANKSGIVING PISS UP

As any sportsman will tell you, having to attend a wedding in the middle of the season is a task that you have to perform occasionally if only to actually stay married. When it comes at a time when you're taking wickets for fun it's even harder, but unless you want to risk your wife walking off into the distance citing unreasonable behaviour and thinking you've been having a lurid affair with ten other blokes on a Saturday from April until September, you just man up and get on the plane.

The wedding in question was for friends called Cristina and Dex and took place in the very pleasant surroundings of a small Italian village called Pontremoli just outside Milan. As the weekend was drawing to a close on a Sunday, there was a lunchtime event high in the hills surrounding the village where I was introduced to one of Cristina's work colleagues from the travel company Trailfinders.

The gentleman's name was Derek Johnston. It appeared clear that he was quite the sports fan, telling me of his work's team amazing travel plans and of all the places they visited around the globe under what looked like the pretence of trying to compete at some tournament or other. There only appeared to be one major setback to their whole plan and that was they were totally and utterly useless.

Derek quickly confessed that he was hoping that he'd be able to convince me to come and join their disparate band of willing but rather unable sportsmen. His opening gambit was fairly straight to the point. "Would you like to come and be our Ringer?" That was obviously enough to get my attention as for the next fifteen minutes, he told me about the Sarasota Thanksgiving Festival in the sunny state of Florida and of the various teams that attended the festivities around the American holiday weekend. The terms were extremely agreeable as well which always helped.

In all honesty, he had me at Florida. The thought of escaping the cold weather for a few days around that time of year was a huge positive and when he managed to get Jacky to agree to let me come out to play the deal was as good as done. The only snag was that there was no chance of attending that year's tournament due to work commitments and so we agreed to stay in touch and became quite good friends to boot, as I awaited the 1999 version of what amounted to a glorified six a side slog fest with more golf than you could throw a stick at.

With the arrival of Lucy in September '99, it also meant that at first we might all come out as a family for a quick holiday. Derek agreed that that wouldn't be an issue but when Jacky decided that it might just be easier for me to go on my own, I didn't really give much thought to the possible travelling dynamic that might have occurred if the Simmonds family had all actually been on the flight from Gatwick to Orlando. This might have had something to do with the fact that seven blokes from Trailfinders plus their ringer were all trashed before the plane had actually left the tarmac at the South Terminal.

Still, the perks of this little jaunt to the USA were becoming immediately obvious. With Trailfinders being British Airways biggest customer, the travelling sports team had somehow managed to burgle eight business class tickets and so this was the first time I'd been able to fly club class and rather nice it was too.

When we arrived in the land of Mickey Mouse, we were catered through to our hotel in Sarasota before the fun started the following morning. With teams from all over the globe, there was a nice feel to the place and the host club had put on a superb show. The great Richie Benaud as their patron, would hand write a new article for the programme every year, which to be fair was a mark of the man.

That said, the standard in that first year was horrifically poor apart from the fact that it appeared that nearly every other team had a version of myself in their sides. Only the team entered by the British Airways pilots seemed to be genuine. Thankfully they didn't let anybody down when it came to people's preconceived ideas about pilots on away days and behaved absolutely appallingly night after night.

With no more than two six a side matches per day, you could smash a quick twenty five and retire and then bowl fast and straight at most of the blokes who were worse than your average village cricketer. Once that was over it was off to the nearest and cheapest golf course before the main attraction for the Trailfinders boys started in the bars and clubs around the town.

The first two years I attended, we made it to the finals before losing out, but for the boys who were regularly getting stuffed out of sight by one bloke year after year, I seemed to have made a difference and I think they enjoyed my contributions. Somehow, I managed to burgle my way out to the annual Sarasota Thanksgiving Festival in 1999, 2000 and 2001 before someone pulled the handbrake up and the fun had to stop.

Sadly, the tournament had started attracting much better teams from the UK as news spread about the many perks that Florida had to offer at that time of the year. In my last year, three Surrey Championship sides took six players from their first teams and made a mockery of some of the sides who kept returning each year for another crack at winning. Still, all good things have to come to and end and by 2002 there really was no need for a ringer with a growing waistline and an average back condition when some teams were turning up with six younger fitter versions of me playing already.

For the Trailfinders boys, they spent the next few years finding more elaborate ways of dining and hacking their way around some of the finest PGA courses that Florida had to offer in the vain hope that their hosts would be featured in next year's brochure. Despite the fact that my golf never actually improved, I had had a fine old time, made some new friends and guess I'll always be grateful that I met the very excellent Derek Johnson one afternoon in the Italian hills.

40

LAST CHANCE FOR GREATNESS

They say you should be at the peak of your cricketing powers between the ages of 27 and 31, still with the ability to bowl at a decent pace but with the added knowledge and experience you've learned along the way. At the ripe old age of 32, I was wondering whether those so-called judges had got it pretty well spot on. Maybe the news that Simmonds number two was on the way at the end of the season made me feel slightly older than I actually was.

With an invitation from Peter Moores to attend the whole of the Sussex pre-season camp at a cold and dreary Hove, I managed to get an enjoyable run out of my own while proving to myself I could still hang in there with the best in the county. The longer the week went on, the better I bowled and, at the end of it, I knew I was a shoe in for the Sussex Board matches coming up.

The season started well for me with a hatful of wickets and it looked like our stay in division two would only last one season. By the end of May, we were comfortably top. I was doing well virtually every time I walked onto the pitch and, generally speaking, the world seemed a happy place. We had another overseas player from Western Province, a lad called Warren Wyngard who hit a clean ball but never really worked out the English pitches and was out lbw hitting across the line so often it became laughable. I was coaching at a lovely school called Great Walstead as well as continuing to work for the cricket department at Hove so the finances appeared to be in pretty good order as well.

The draw for the second round of the Nat West Trophy had paired us with the strong minor counties side of Hertfordshire with the winners getting the plum draw of a home tie against Lancashire. I'd be lying if I said the thought of running down the hill at Hove to bowl to a line-up that included Atherton, Crawley, Fairbrother and a young Andrew Flintoff didn't excite me but I wasn't so sure I'd have wanted to face their Sri Lankan overseas player Murali, as I wouldn't have had a clue what was coming, He would undoubtedly have made me look like a clueless arse, but then he did that time and time again to far better players than me. For people like me and my team mates, such a match would be the chance to walk out onto the big stage and witness firsthand what it's like to stand next to someone who really knows what they are doing. It would be our version of the third round of the FA Cup and with it the dreams of heroics and the chance to replay the DVD time and time again with a headline grabbing giant killing.

Before we could deal with such issues, we had the pleasure of staying at a nice Holiday Inn type establishment just outside the M25 ahead of our match against Hertfordshire. We had a good side, made up of some of the best cricketers in the leagues as well as our overseas player – the opening bowler Shane Jurgensen, from Western Australia – and a young Mike Yardy, who, ten years later, would go on to get a T20 World Cup winner's medal.

The match itself was a tense affair where we never capitalized on a brilliant 90 from Mark Newell and, at one stage, it looked like we were going to be bowled out painfully short of a good total. When I strolled in at No 11 and hit my first three balls cleanly through the covers for four, I wondered, along with everyone else watching, why the hell was I batting so low? No 11? Surely not! Everything I hit flew off the middle and, if the overs hadn't run out, I'd have surely broken all batting records instead of a decent 18 not out. Still, we had some sort of total to defend and, with a decent attack and an Aussie who had bowled the touring English side out that winter, what could possibly go wrong? As it happened, quite a lot actually, as the wayward Jurgensen flew to all parts of the ground in his first three overs and the dreams of Lancashire at home looked to be vanishing in the same way as England's hopeless 1999 World Cup campaign on home soil a few days earlier.

As Hertfordshire got off to a flyer, my stunning 18 not out was about to look utterly meaningless when the ball was thrown to me. Thankfully, I picked up a couple of wickets for virtually nothing to get us back into the game and, at the three-quarter stage, the match was evenly poised and while I was grazing on the boundary I was starting to think about whether, if I could add another wicket or two in my next spell, it would be the done thing to pocket the £900 gold award all for myself. The game turned when the young off spinner Jon Newell – Mark's brother – dropped a seemingly easy caught and bowled that looped over his shoulder and, looking like a drunk man running in treacle, he managed to spill it. It was such a shame as Jon had bowled so well throughout, keeping the rate down and us in the game. But a player like David Ward, the ex-Surrey batsman, was not going to miss out on such a reprieve and, in a shift of gears, he tore into the attack in a five-over spell where everyone including little old me, was sent to all parts of the ground. He made their victory look a fairly comfortable one, ending up 98 not out, pocketing the money and looking forward to the next round. In truth, I'd had a pretty good game, close to a match winning one for 90 per cent of the time, but ex pros Ward and Mark Newell had looked a class apart and the dreams of the biggest match of most of our lives had gone up in smoke.

Driving home, the mood in the car was a pretty sombre one with all the regrets and could-have-beens that make the difference between success and failure. Should we have played a stronger side with more ex pros? Should we have drunk less the night before and hit the sack earlier than the less-than-professional two or three o clock we eventually turned in? For some, there would be other chances to play in such games again, but for others, including me, it was clear that the years might count against us in the future.

Over the next few weeks, I sometimes thought we'd get the chance to play it all over again and change history for the better but then reality would kick in and remind me that things weren't meant to be and the opportunity had passed us all by. The matches all had the feeling of "After the Lord Mayor's Show" and, in truth I found the next set of Board matches uneventful and time consuming, especially with a toddler at home and another one on the way.

To make matters worse, the season took a considerable downturn when my injury hoodoo struck again and this time it wasn't destined to be a short-term problem. During a spell against Middleton, just at the point of delivery, I felt my back seize up as if someone had drained all the oil from my engine and then decided to see whether it would still run smoothly. It didn't. It was as if a large steel plate had been inserted inside my cricket whites and I'd been asked to be as flexible as possible. Over the years I'd been good at playing through the pain barrier with the help of more than a few pills and bandages. With hindsight, I should have taken the rest of the season off to deal with the problem but, like many foolish people, I tried week by week to get through the matches and surprisingly wondered why I was getting nowhere. The trouble is that, if you've been used to being the mainstay of the attack and thrived on the fact that everyone relied on you to do the lion's share of wicket taking, then your pride and king-sized ego think you'll still be able to do the business on sheer reputation alone. As I was to find out, that did not happen very often. In truth, from that moment, I would never be able to bowl as quickly again.

I was in pain for weeks, popping pills like they were Smarties and getting more and more frustrated as the team's results got worse and we slipped further down the league. Members and players started to think I'd pulled up the ladder and wasn't interested any more, especially with all the other things going on in my life. After all I'd done over the previous six or seven seasons it was another moment when you wonder if clubs really do deserve any of their players to show any kind of loyalty whatsoever. You only have to read *Animal Farm* as a schoolchild to realise you go from being the jewel in the crown one minute to heading for the knacker's yard the next, once your usefulness wears off.

As a result, we failed to gain promotion and so another season in division two beckoned. My stellar form during the first half of the season meant I still ended up with a good tally as the prizes were handed out but, in truth, it mattered little as I prepared for a long winter of recovery and visits to the physio, injections and more needles than an embroidery shop. The best piece of news by a country mile was that, on September 21, 1999, the beautiful

Lucy Jane Simmonds was born, in somewhat easier circumstances than her older sister, in the Princess Royal, Haywards Heath and so now there were two little daddy's girls to look after and to juggle all the things that were going on in our lives. When it came to reading bed time stories, you began to see the bigger picture and questioned whether it really mattered that you had the stiffest back in Sussex and that plenty of people thought you'd lost your mojo.

41

MASTERING THE ART OF WORKING FOR NOTHING

One of the things I did manage to learn at college was that, in the real world, some nine out of every ten new businesses go belly up within the first three years. A small percentage are still running successfully a further three years down the line but you can still fail at any time so, in truth, you really do wonder why you bother in the first place. Well I did, indeed, try and, for my troubles, I ended up working for the bank, the accountants and, best of all, the Inland Revenue. As margins grew tighter and the fixed costs needed to be paid, I considered several options before coming up with an idea towards the end of my stay in Cape Town back in 1997 that I hoped would make me a wealthy man and bring my dreams of world domination one step closer.

The stocking filler Christmas present of that year for many young South Africans was a plastic coaching ball, nicely packaged up and sold all over the country in supermarkets as well as sports shops. It was brightly coloured and had different finger positions for the various grips needed for swing and seam and it sold by the truckload. It seemed that almost every child had one and so I came up with the bright idea of trying something similar for a bat. There would be bright stickers to help with some sensible coaching points and a special rubber grip to help with the position of your hands. Like a man possessed, I became that little boy watching Blue Peter and went to work with paper, scissors and sticky back plastic and came up with a prototype that even made Mrs Simmonds and our landlord think I was onto something. Before I left, I had a designer make me a better version and when I got home I patented the idea and registered the intellectual property to stop some scheming businessman making it themselves and running off into the sunset with all the cash.

I went to get some advice from Roger Myall, a friend who played for Eastbourne, who had recently started working for Newbery as their sales manager. My thought was that the bat would look better with a reputable sticker on it rather than something that I'd knocked up on my PC and so, after he was impressed with the idea, we struck up a partnership of sorts and went off to see all the equipment manufacturers one by one. I decided that I'd rather make less of a cut selling thousands than make more but only sell a few hundred and, for a while, I really did have the hope that this idea might actually work.

It was while meeting all the companies that I realised that some of them really were small players in a very small cottage industry and, despite their ambitions, nearly all of them concluded that, for this to work, it had to be supported by one of the big boys, either Slazenger or Gray Nicolls. Others like Gunn and Moore, Kookaburra, Hunts County thought the idea had potential but they didn't have enough of the market share to fully capitalise on the product's potential. They all, however, warned us that the idea could be stolen and produced by someone else – and that wouldn't have been the first time it had happened.

With this advice, we decided we would only show the bat to companies who would sign a legal document promising not to copy the idea, something which, to my amazement, Grays refused to do which meant we left their offices without showing them what we'd gone all the way down to Robertsbridge to try and sell. No coconut there then.

On the other hand, Slazenger were incredibly helpful and, under new sales director Sean Morris, the ex-Hampshire player, had invested a huge amount of money in cricket prior to the 1999 World Cup, getting some of the biggest names in the game to use and endorse their products. The best thing was that, with their brand behind it, Sean thought the idea had huge potential and, for a small amount of time, Mr Simmonds and Mr Myall sat across the table trying not to grin about what the future could hold. Sean Morris started talking about a campaign that had Graeme Hick, Alec Stewart and Andrew Flintoff covering England, Mark Waugh fronting the Australian market and Jacques Kallis and the Flower brothers doing the same in Africa. A meeting was arranged for a month later where we would discuss the finer points. As we left the offices, we both looked at each other and secretly yelped like poorer versions of Del Boy and Rodney after they'd finally hit the jackpot. This time next year, Roger my son, we'll be millionaires . . .

In the following weeks, when I lay in the bath at night, I thought of the many different ways to spend my yearly royalty cheque as the bat sold to generations of young children throughout the cricket-playing universe and, to be honest, it was an awful lot of fun. However, like a lot of dreams, there was no happy ending. You see, some bright bean counter at Dunlop Slazenger HQ had realised that spending many hundreds of thousands of pounds putting the world's best players on overpriced long term contacts to use your equipment in the hope that you'd shift a lot more equipment ranked alongside the C5 and the Betamax video as dire business decisions of our time. Suddenly, all bets were off and the chances of my coaching bat making me a rich man decreased by 100 per cent. If I remember correctly, the word "bollocks" came around the same time as my forehead slumped and hit the top of the office desk as I came to terms with the fact that I was still skint and had a non-profit making sports business that was making me ill.

My only option was to try and market the bat myself. With the help of a designer, I came up with some eye catching looks and, with Roger's help, got the bats and the rubbers made in India and shipped to the UK where I planned to sell them through the shop and on the internet. So, one large VAT bill later, the Super Striker was born and there still seemed a small beacon of hope that they might become successful enough for me to escape to a large house with a pool somewhere in the sun.

In an effort to get some endorsements, I went to the ECB offices at Lord's and saw Hugh Morris the ex-England opener who, before he became a central part of the new Team England, was in charge of youth development. Of all the hundreds of people I saw around the country and of all the children in schools I used for market research, the one and only person who didn't like it was Mr Morris. His two assistants thought it was great but not Mr Morris. Two days later, I took it to the annual Coaches Association conference at the NEC in Birmingham where Peter Moores, Mickey Stewart and the-then England coach Duncan Fletcher liked what they saw. To this day, somewhere in the depths of my study, I have a signed letter from Mr Fletcher which kindly says "Really clever idea. I'm sure the kids will love it. All the best of luck with the venture, Duncan Fletcher." So, the England coach thinks it's got potential but no company will get behind it.

The sad thing about the whole story was that I sold every single bat I brought into the country but the costs for such small numbers were too high to continue. For all the effort, as well as the fleeting dreams of fame and fortune, I was now probably a few grand out of pocket, but what's a few grand more when you're already losing a bucket load of cash each year?

42

PLANNING FOR
RETIREMENT FIRST
TIME AROUND

I once heard a phrase regarding retirement which went something like this: *It's better for them to ask you why you have, rather than hear them ask you why you haven't.* With that in mind, I often wondered why I kept going and what life would be like if I didn't do it any more. With two toddlers to look after, your natural focus shifts and, without realising it, the hunger and desire you once had, and which drove you on, starts to evaporate.

In order to cling on to the top end of club life, I would have the girls early on Saturday morning so Jacky could sleep before I headed off. My major problem, though, was that the only thing that seemed to keep Hannah happy long enough for me to feed Lucy was a large talking purple dinosaur called Barney who would become the bane of my life. As many parents will tell you, the image of this sickly sweet animal was enough to make you vomit. Watching this politically correct T Rex run around with his friends, all made up from the different creeds and colours of society while singing catchy melodies about pizza and trips to the zoo, meant that I heard them so often they hung around in my head like the Lord's Prayer. Sometimes, as I stood at the top of my mark, hard new ball in hand, instead of feeling aggressive and ready for action, all I could hear was that f'ng dinosaur telling me how much he loved me and singing that we were all such a happy family. Hannah and Lucy may have loved watching him but it nearly drove me to the brink of despair and in need of some serious therapy. I once even imagined that one of the batsmen actually was Barney and spent the next few overs trying my hardest to remove his head from his shoulders for all the pain and suffering that purple bastard had caused me.

As the next few seasons passed, I still enjoyed some good days but there were an increasing number of average ones as well, so much so that several members told me that I wasn't playing as well as I used to and they weren't too impressed by excuses of a young family and a less than prosperous business. As someone once said, there is not much difference between a pat on the back and a clip round the ear and that was certainly how it seemed at times. There will always be someone younger and quicker to come along and start to take the plaudits and, whatever you do and wherever you go, no one's time lasts for ever. You must be careful not to overstay your welcome. In sides I'd played in, players who had once been forces had lost that power and become shadows of themselves while, year by year, some of the regular faces on the circuit would disappear, lost to the golf course or, worse still, the dreaded Saturday ritual of the shopping centre or even the sports centre play areas.

There was one image around that time that has always stuck in my mind. As a side Chichester had been arguably the premier side in Sussex and a force nationally for some time. Their side were so strong it seemed like playing against a first class outfit but they were all around the same age, growing older together until time caught up with them. In their ranks they had an Australian called Neil Budden, a quite superb bowler. Tall and immensely skilful, he had such brilliant control that it was an honour to play against him. If you were smart, you could learn so much from him and, in his pomp, every match was a bowling master class. However he had hung around one season too long and, playing against him in a rain affected match, Peter Mills and I decided he'd lost it and, after all the grief he'd given us over the years, it was now time to at least have some small payback. For the next four overs, we smashed him to all parts and it was quite sad to see a player I'd respected so much walk slowly with his hat down to fine leg. He wasn't the first person it would happen to, and he certainly wouldn't be the last, but it did make you sit up and realise that, whether you liked it or not, this was a fate that awaited many players.

So, as I entered the 2003 season and aged 36, I thought I should get out while way ahead on points. For the first time in ages we had a strong side, had recruited wisely and, with the addition of Zimbabwean all-rounder Richard Sims, looked to have all of the bases covered, certainly when it came to that time honoured blend of youth and experience. His century in the first match at Brighton set the tone for the season and, although we went through some changes, we never looked back and, for the first time in all years I'd played, we had become a team to be feared or, at the very least, respected. We probably drew a couple too many games but the weather really screwed us up as we had at least three more matches called off than the other title challengers which was a shame as many good judges felt our side was as good as any over the years. What was interesting to see was how quickly sides could change from incredibly strong to average and below and vice versa with only with a couple of personnel changes.

The game against Eastbourne was particularly satisfying. There were players in our team who had been around long enough to remember Eastbourne players screaming abuse from the balcony during their pomp back in the middle to late 1990s. Strangely, they were not so quick to voice their opinions when we had them at 0 for five and then 8 for seven before finally hammering them by ten wickets, soon after thrashing them in the away fixture earlier in the season. How things had changed and a mental note to those who genuinely believe in what goes around, comes around.

When Sims was called up to play in the ODI series against England and South Africa, he was replaced by his compatriot Mark Vermeulen, who added strength to the batting line up and quite a different angle to the dressing room. In later years he would have his problems both mentally and physically but we took to him and enjoyed his company. He could play, too, which always helps, but it was clear for all to see he might have been at least a couple of loaves short of a full picnic. Back then we thought he was on the right side of nicely bonkers but others might have since formed a different opinion.

As the season was coming to a close, it suddenly hit me that it would be a good time to call it quits and walk off into the sunset. I didn't much like the attitude of some of the younger players and the way they spoke about a couple of my friends still in the side was hard to take. Perhaps I was like them when I was their age but I still didn't like it and I had no doubt they would talk about me in the same vein once I'd stopped producing the goods. Whether that would be next season or the following one, who knows, but it would still happen.

We finished fourth in the league, a travesty for the talent we had, but I ended up with over 40 wickets at under ten and second spot in the county averages – not bad for an old git with a creaky back, worsening knees and a dreadful left ankle. I'd announced my retirement but was there a guard of honour, or a celebratory dinner, a reception or even a piss up in the changing room? Of course there wasn't. Did I expect there to be? Of course I didn't although, if I'm honest, a little bit of appreciation for all the hard work would have been nice. They probably thought my retirement would last about as long as some fighter who decided to return and, to be fair, they had a point. Like many things in life, it's all about timing and deciding when to clear off for good certainly falls into that category.

43

OHHH VIENNA

When you spend most of your day sitting at the computer hoping that someone might actually buy something of value or in reality wasting way too much time looking at ways to escape from your woes, then when yet another begging email comes in to your inbox, it's normally greeted by sending it straight to the trash basket.

However, this time the email in question looked somewhat different in that it wasn't from a spotty fifteen year old telling me what a superb prospect he was and I'd be mad not to give him loads of free kit in return for, well nothing actually. This time it came from a man called Duncan Kendal who was asking for some coloured shirts for his touring indoor side who were playing in some tournament in Vienna of all places. Thankfully I was quite intrigued and so replied by asking him to call the office and tell me more.

When the telephone rang he was obviously quite a salesman, but seemed at the outset to be quite a decent bloke. His touring side, the Teeside Polygons were made up from lads who went to the polytechnic back in the day, plus some club players from the Hertfordshire area where he now lived. He impressed on me that the competition was genuine and that the two winners of the ECB national finals got a free invite as well as several sides from the UK and Europe. It was also a chance to sell some equipment to the clubs where kit was hard to come by and they all needed a good internet based company that could supply them with the things they needed during the season.

It all seemed a fairly good idea when Mr Kendal suggested that it might be worth my while coming out with some bats at least and setting up a mobile shop and seeing if I could sell some and at the end of a very pleasant conversation he asked whether I played myself. By Monday morning he'd been back on the phone and persuaded me to bring some playing kit and trainers as I was now in their side. Thankfully Jacky bought me a return ticket to Vienna for my birthday and I was all set to visit somewhere where there is a very nice opera house. My side of the bargain was to knock them up some polo shirts to play in and then make one for myself as well.

Now apparently the other members of the side were less understanding when Duncan told them of the deal he'd struck and they all came equipped with their own shirts just in case this fraudster didn't get anyway near Heathrow Airport. They were even taking bets whether I'd pitch up and so Duncan stood to lose some cash if I didn't materialise. They'd even done some checking on the Cricinfo website to see that I actually existed.

So in bleak mid February, I made my ways with all sorts of baggage, including the playing shirts to the airport and boarded the plane to Vienna. When I arrived, I took a taxi to the hotel in slight bewilderment at what I was actually doing. This could be the biggest waste of time with some blokes who I don't even really know and plenty of others who I didn't know whether I would even like. When I arrived at the hotel, Duncan had left some kit in my room, clearly still hopeful that I'd turn up along with the address of the bar they were drinking at. So once showered, I jumped into another cab and took the bizarre trip to a random bar in downtown Vienna where I would see what all the fuss was about. When I finally arrived, I stood outside in the bitter cold, when I noticed that there was a lot of noise coming from the bar with what sounded like two guitars going off. Not only was I miles away from home, freezing my nads off in the middle of winter, but the people I've come to meet are all from the god squad and happily strumming away to classics such as "kum ba yah" and "my sweet lord".

Once I'd plucked up the courage and entered the bar, a very relieved Duncan Kendal greeted me like the man who had just won some money betting and thankfully his mates were all extremely good lads. Come the end of the evening I was completely slaughtered as well as singing myself hoarse. Hotel California probably never sounded better.

The next morning, upon arrival at the sports hall where the action was due to take place over the next two days, it appeared that the standard of the players taking part would actually be quite high and that the two sides from the ECB finals, Durham University, including a young James Foster who would find fame with Essex and Pudsey St Lawrence from Yorkshire were proper teams. My team was made up of some players who'd played minor counties and good club cricketers and so we'd stand a chance if the hangovers could disappear in time. I managed to bowl straight at the stumps and not disgrace myself and the company was of the highest standard.

In the evening, there was a dinner where each team had to give a speech thanking the hosts for the effort they'd put in and

Duncan did a fine job in making everyone laugh at the correct moments. It seemed that our main job was to be quite good at playing indoor cricket until it was time to exit the competition and then getting the guitars out when everyone was suitably drunk and having a sing song. Pissed again and even more hoarse. As we ventured into Vienna in the early hours of Saturday night, the drinking continued until we eventually hit the pillows by which time any hope of a decent performance on the Sunday were quickly diminishing.

Over breakfast the next morning, the conversation seemed to centre around just how much eight hundred euros was if you converted it into pounds. That was because some prat had brought some bottles of dreadful champagne at a bar and it was heading for his credit card. The feeling was that it was slightly more than he'd realised at the time.

The competition was entering the semi final stage where we had somehow made it through to face the hosts Vienna CC. They were made up of some ex pats from different parts of the world, a couple of local lads and an Englishman who seemed to be at odds with the rest of the tournament but everyone seemed to tolerate him because he came along with a very attractive wife. Men really can be so shallow at times. For Vienna, the competition was a big deal and faced with six hungover middle aged men from England surely gave them the upper hand. They even brought along a sports psychiatrist, which seemed like they were surely taking it a bit too seriously. However, they shouldn't have bothered as their plans managed to backfire as the mighty Polygons marched comfortably into the finals where they were sure to be smashed to all parts of the large sports hall by the ECB National Champions, Pudsey St Lawrence.

We got nowhere near to getting the total we needed but the lads seemed to be happy that they'd performed better than the form book suggested they might. The presentation and raffles were truly comical and the choice of Hooters for the final evening of the weekend made the trip even more surreal. I had managed to sell quite a few bats, get some excellent contacts and enjoyed myself beyond belief. With Messer's Thewlis, Hodge, Pearce, Robinson and Kendal it was hard not to. They might sound like a firm of solicitors but they had entertained me brilliantly all weekend to the extent that I even started to look at the prospect of getting a guitar. Its their fault that I now own several.

With my position as honorary Polygon now secured, we attended the yearly European Winter Cup each February with only the standard of hotel causing concern amongst the ranks. Now Michael Thewlis might be a good cricketer, fine guitarist and all round excellent bloke, but he was truly hopeless when it came to organising the sleeping arrangements. Each year the standard of hotels got worse until it reached a point where we could sink no lower. When you give the taxi driver the address of where you're staying and he asks why the hell are you staying there, then you know that you're not expecting the pull up outside the Ritz. It's fair to say that depending on what you're looking for in a hotel, then one with no stars whatsoever is not where you'd be hoping to reside for the weekend.

With general apathy raging amongst the Polygon when we checked in, the busty receptionist with long blond hair gleefully took all of our passports for safe keeping and gave us the keys to somewhere with no lift and in some cases no curtains in the rooms outside a huge neon sign that might as well have spelt shithole in Austrian. It was however, in the morning when the alarms bells started to ring. The staff all looked similar except for the fact that they all had different coloured hair from the night we checked in and to say that some of the clients staying at the hotel seemed rather dubious, especially when it came to their dress sense would have been an understatement. We put it down to the fact that they were European after all and nowhere near as trendy as their English visitors.

If the alarm bells were ringing on Saturday morning, by Sunday they were clanging as loudly as they possibly could. When you are greeted by the busty reception who had long blond hair on Friday night, you don't expect her to now have Black hair and to be dressed up as Snow White, whilst two small men run behind her dressed as Happy and Sneezy. God only know where the other five dwarfs were. When I enquired about the change in appearance, she informed me that the clients were paying good money for her services and so that was what she was wearing that morning. Chaps, I think we're staying in a brothel, which is always a good place to leave your passports for the weekend. We genuinely expected to be regularly contacted by Interpol finding out what our forged passports had been getting up to in the seedy underbelly of the various European capitals.

With the role of accommodation organiser passed on to someone less woeful the following year, the slightly more palatial surroundings obviously seemed to do the trick as for the first time the Polygons went all the way to the final and to their great surprise actually won the Winter Cup. As a way of celebrating our new trophy we announced at the Hooters dinner that we were retiring on top and therefore wouldn't be bringing any players let alone any guitars back the following year to defend the trophy.

Over the next two years we played a tournament in the Czech Republic, which Michael's brother Martin had organised, losing in the final to some team from France and then in our final year of touring had the pleasure of trying Ice Cricket in Estonia. You would think that if you're going to play on ice, then there will actually be some ice around to actually play on, but when we were told that it was too warm for the competition to be played then that's a long way to go to have to play with an incrediball on an AstroTurf, somewhere outside of the capital. We managed to win it that too, making us probably the most successful English side in Europe after Liverpool and Nottingham Forest in the 1970's. However, the guitars weren't welcome anywhere in the city and the fact that there were stag parties everywhere and we kept being approached by all sorts women trying to get us to buy them for the night or for a better rate, the whole weekend, made our return very unlikely.

So the golden years of European indoor cricket had come to an end as we were all getting older, creaking more than we used to and it was becoming less likely for our wives to let us bugger off for the weekend to behave like small children somewhere on foreign soil. Still, as I still see them this day, normally in the Harris gardens at Lords, I really am truly thankful that I did reply to Mr Kendal's somewhat random email. Funnily enough, we never did get to visit the Opera House.

44

ACADEMY LIFE WITH SOME FAMOUS FACES THROWN IN

It wasn't the first time I'd made a large life decision after a bol
locking but, this time, I was pleased someone had taken me to
task. I'm not even sure which parent it was but he didn't hold
back. Why, he asked, was a professional level 3 coach trying to
sell cricket equipment while the children outside in the sunshine
were being taught by a grunting sixth form student who plays in
the fourth team? He didn't stop there and, try as I might to
explain myself, it made no difference. Mr Angry from Tunbridge
Wells had had his rant and, to be fair, his annual subscription of
about £20.00 more than allowed him to speak to everyone in that
manner. The trouble was that, if I was being completely honest,
nearly everything he said made perfect sense.

That evening, after the ritual of bath and bedtime stories, I sat down at the dining room table with a pen and paper and started to scribble. How could I change how the basics of coaching had been for the previous 20 years? Thankfully the scribbling continued and, by the time Midsomer Murders was about to start, I had the basics for the East Grinstead Cricket Academy. The next day, with the iron still hot so to speak, I drove to Hove and persuaded Steve Peyman, the county's youth development officer, to let me have full control of East Grinstead and its surrounding villages. I would organise and run a programme aimed at primary and secondary schools that linked in with the town's major club and the smaller village outfits because, as I saw it, many of the most successful players to play for East Grinstead had actually started out as village cricketers. Steve gave the plans his full backing and was very supportive of everything we tried to do.

The hardest thing was to convince some of the club members that this was the way forward and, even though they agreed with it in principle, there was always the underlying issue of how it would be funded. As in so many clubs all over the country, there is an archaic notion that nobody, no matter how qualified, should be allowed to make any sort of living from running this type of venture. Hedge funds, private equity, property development and, if you believed some people, cricket coaching were the way forward when it came to serious wealth creation. I'm sure that many parents have decided to send their child to an expensive private school in the hope that one day it will all pay off and they'll make it big in the ultra competitive world of cricket coaching.

With the generous donations and loans from a handful of club members, I had enough of a buffer to get started and so, early in 2004, the school programme began, fitting in with holiday courses and private sessions that would keep the cash flowing and, more importantly, the children coming through the door. Top range equipment was purchased and used by both academy and club members and a thriving new venture was up and running.

As well as the coaching opportunities, there were funding schemes available through Sport England and links with the business community that meant it was starting to become a full time job and, as well as the usual golf days and dinners, I felt we needed a focal point to sell the academy to the companies that had invested in me. To achieve this, I came up with the idea of hosting a celebrity cricket match against Lashings, often touted as the Harlem Globetrotters of cricket, who would, for the right fee, be happy to bring their roadshow to your town. Although they had an impressive list of players on their books, the problem was that you never quite knew who was going to turn out. As we waited for final confirmation on star names, we started selling tickets for the match and for a dinner. Such a big event had never been hosted by the club before and, with every school child in the area getting a free ticket, we were praying that the outlay for the match at least would be covered. If it went badly, our venture could have been dead in the water before the first youngsters came through the door. Picking a side to take on Lashings was also proving difficult as the changing room bitchiness grew and some people's egos went into overdrive to the extent that you wondered whether it was all worth it in the first place.

As it turned out, some companies and individuals were incredibly helpful with their time and their chequebooks but our main bit of good fortune came through the people at Channel 4 who were covering Test cricket at the time. They were looking to do a piece for the interval at the following Test about West Indian cricket so, without notice, the side turning up at our big day read like a who's who of Caribbean greats. Joel Garner, Courtney Walsh, Alvin Kallicharran, Vasbert Drakes, Sherwin Campbell, Stuart Williams and the great man himself, Sir Vivian Richards, were all there. Added to the line-up were Grant Flower, Greg Blewett, Shahid Afridi and Rashid Latif and the New Zealander Chris Harris. It was some line-up for the cameras to film and for us to play against, to say the least. The crowd and the corporates would be thrilled but, because the final names came through so late, I had no time to announce the details to the press and boost attendance.

August 4, 2004 was a beautifully sunny day, ideal to showcase the club and the new cricket academy. The crowds came, the marquees were full and the ground looked a picture. The match was watchable as well and I even chipped in with a few wickets, which was a nice bonus. However, the absolute highlight was seeing Sir Vivian walk out to bat with that undeniable swagger that, even in his late fifties, still took the crowd's breath away. As I stood in the outfield it dawned on me that I'd been lucky enough to have played against and stood next to some truly great players, but this was Viv Richards, the man who had struck an unforgettable hundred in the first match I'd seen live, the 1979 World Cup Final at Lord's. He was one of the five men honoured by Wisden as cricketers of the century and, today, he was only yards away from me on an actual cricket field. He might have been older and greyer, but this man could arguably be the greatest batter of all time. If people think you have a claim on that title, then you have certainly left quite a footprint on history.

With Lashings taking the victory that everyone expected, the festivities continued long into the night as players delighted the crowds with their stories that, although people might have heard them before, always sounded better when they came out of the mouths of the legends themselves. For a first attempt, it couldn't really have gone better. All the interested parties made some money and, I guess, my stock was fairly high. Within months the first children came through the gates as we tried to get as many as possible to play the game as well as keeping an eye out for the better ones who looked like they had the ability to play at a decent level. The word quickly spread as other clubs and sports tried to copy what we were doing. As they say, imitation is the sincerest form of flattery.

The following year we decided to have an early season official opening and so, to add to the now annual Lashings World XI fixture at the end of the season, I was delighted to persuade a full strength Sussex side to take on a full strength Lashings XI as part of Mark Robinson's testimonial and, better still, got Sir Garry Sobers to officially open the academy. He was a charming man and great company – all we had to do was prize him away from the local bookies in time. Again, tickets and marquees were sold, people flocked to see the players and Lashings didn't disappoint, bringing players like Herschelle Gibbs and Chris Cairns to add to their already stacked celebrity XI. An enjoyable lunch gave me the chance to sell my ideas to a celebrity packed audience and it was good to hear the complimentary things people were saying about what we'd achieved in such a short time.

A crowd of 1,400 watched the cricket – not 3,000 as reported in the local press which, at £10 a ticket, gave some people the chance to assume we'd made £30,000; sadly, we did not. To see a cricketing knight of the realm cut the ribbon to open the academy in front of hundreds of our students all decked out in their clothing, and with the Sussex and Lashings players behind them, was full vindication of all the hard work that had gone into the event. In addition, to see your father chatting to Sir Garry Sobers, one of his cricketing heroes, in a private marquee was the icing on the cake of what was a pretty good day. Even South East News covered the event on TV, splashing my suntanned nose all over the telly and showing everyone what a arse I was for having my sunglasses on my head throughout my interview. They could have told me as I honestly had forgotten and, after the event, I had plenty of texts telling me to take them off. Never mind, I was still a TV star.

More events were planned, thousands of children were coached, many of whom would go on to play for local sides with some going into the East Grinstead first team. People were employed, a tour to Cape Town went off relatively smoothly – if you don't count nearly losing two pissed up lads running around the V and A waterfront and getting hammered out of sight by the various sides we played – and, until around 2008, things were looking good. But, as is often the case, the good times were not going to last. The first problem was that, with the Olympics heading to London in 2012, sports funding started to dry up. Added to that, four years down the line, people were becoming bored with the Lashings matches. I was also beginning to despair at the ridiculous expectations of some parents when it came to their children's actual ability. That, and the continual backstabbing from club members, meant the fun had stated to wear off and it was the beginning of the end as far as I was concerned of what was in essence a great project, years ahead of its time.

If I've come across as slightly bitter and twisted in this chapter then you'd be right in thinking that at times running the whole project often left me extremely pissed off. I never ceased to be amazed about how ungrateful some people could be for all the good we produced in such as short amount of time. We put on events that had never been put on before or since and improved facilities and structures beyond recognition. As there has been a huge fall in the number of youngsters playing cricket locally in the last few years, perhaps it wasn't as easy as some people thought it would be. Maybe, just maybe, we just might have been good at what we did but then again, as everyone knows, anyone with half a brain can coach sport – it's really like taking money for old jam. There you have it, rant over.

45

THE HOME OF CRICKET

Ever since I'd walked into the place when I was 12 years old, I was desperate to play there. Every single time I sat down or watched at the nets, saw the players walk across the ground and back into the famous pavilion I was desperate to have a go. More than anywhere else in the world, I wanted to play at Lord's.

Compared with most people, I'd been pretty blessed with some of the grounds I'd played on but, for any cricket lover, Lord's stands apart. My father had been a member since the mid-1970s and he kindly put me on the waiting list on my 18th birthday, more in hope than anticipation as it can be an awfully long time before the letter comes from the secretary telling you that you are in. In fact, at normal rates, I would still probably be on the waiting list today. It seemed that only the prospect of becoming England captain or maybe Prime Minister would bump me up the list before I turned 60. The only good thing about not being a member was that the gold and orange tie never really took my fancy although, I'm glad to say, a slightly more toned down navy blue version is now available.

However, you could become a playing member which made the whole prospect far more palatable and, after some form filling and a decent supporting letter from the lovely and much missed Sandy Ross, I'd managed to start playing for MCC in the summer of 1996. As the average age of the playing staff was pretty high, anyone who was able to run in and bowl with any sort of pace was always likely to be welcomed with open arms. It was also the best way to make plenty of new mates, maybe get on one of the famous tours and, if you're lucky enough, blag a match at the most famous cricket ground in the world.

By the winter of 2004, I'd been on a few tours and played in quite a few regional matches but the news I had waited for since 1979 finally came through the post just before Christmas with mixed results. It seemed like a cruel twist of fate that I'd been chosen to play for South East at the exact same time that I'd picked up the worst back injury of my life. Even at that stage I felt that the cricketing gods were not on my side and I phoned the captain to tell him I couldn't play. Thankfully he was having none of it and he told me that, whatever happened, I was playing and to get fit. So I spent a fortune seeing every possible back cracker, back bender and spiritual healer out there and, aided by numerous stick-on heat patches, I set about travelling to the hotel opposite in St John's Wood the night before the match.

The side were made up of several of the best players I had played with or against in the Sussex League over the years who, like me, were getting slightly past their sell-by date but were still able to occasionally do themselves justice when needed. The walk to the ground, into the pavilion, past the pictures of famous players and officials and into the home dressing room was about as thrilling a walk as you can get. It had been a while since I had played in a changing room with an attendant but the prospect of towels, drinks and any help for a crocked old fast bowler with a genuinely average lower back was gratefully received. All of us were lapping up the experience and wondering what it must be like on a big match day with a full house. I was like a dog with two dicks. The walk through the pavilion and across the ground to the Nursery End brought home all the history that had gone before and also showed just how sloped the ground really was, once you were standing in the middle.

For me, the nets were a struggle and became more of a photo opportunity for all concerned as three players from East Grinstead past and present had their pictures taken. For Sandy Ross, ex captain and a good friend of mine for many years, this was the stuff of dreams. Now I love cricket, but nowhere near as much as this man and now he was realising a dream by getting to bowl the first ball of the match. For a bloke who could talk for a living he could barely speak. When he sadly died a few years later in 2009, you knew he would have been proud to have achieved that life-long ambition.

When it came for me to bowl, to say I started gingerly would be an understatement and the fielders saved me from a hammering in the first couple of overs. Thankfully my back eased up to the extent that I managed to bowl a decent spell and got the first wicket of the day when ex Warwickshire batter Dave Banks played all round one to have his middle stump removed, giving me a cricketing high like few I'd known before. I know they probably had watered the base but my name was on the scoreboard in bright lights and that would do me, thank you very much. After the winter I'd endured I knew I would stiffen up after one spell and so at lunch I took full advantage of the famous Lord's canteen and, like the rest of the side, ate until I could barely walk. No wonder so many of the Middlesex players were on the larger side.

If I'd played there full time it would have been back to the days of fatties like Colin Milburn and WG Grace. I'd have given Mike Gatting a run for his money, too.

As I was batting at No 6 and we had a few decent players in before me, I took the chance to enjoy a phrase that not many get to hear. When the attendant comes to you and says that he understands you've been having some back issues over the winter and would I like him to "draw me a warm bath"? The answer to that was a not surprising " Errr Yes please" and then, when he asks whether you would like to read the Telegraph, Independent or the Daily Mail while in there, then you know that having a butler at home must be a bloody good gig. You're at Lord's lad, so obviously no offers of the Sun or the Mirror and quite right too.

Upon exiting one of the great baths of our time, I had to pad up and pretend to look like the batsman that I occasionally could be. With a quick flurry of wickets and with us well behind the huge total we were facing, I made my way past the pictures of what seemed to be a hundred previous England captains through the Long Room where a couple of well wishers gave me their best and then through the gates and out onto the hallowed grass. Now I know this match had nothing on it and that I'd played in far more important matches previously, but my complete focus was not to balls up and get nought. Under no circumstances whatsoever was I to get a first baller at Lord's.

Several big lunges meant that the first ball was kept out and then, when the kind man bowled one on my legs, I managed to flick it off my hip Mark Waugh-style down to fine leg for three priceless runs that meant I had avoided my second-worst nightmare. As the run rate climbed and wickets fell I managed to hang in there while most of my decent shots hit fielders and my thoughts turned to those who might have wanted a go as well. Thankfully three boundaries came in three balls, all making a beautiful bullet sounds as they crashed into the boundary boards. What it must be like to do that against Donald, Warne or Akram, heaven only knows. When I'd reached the decent-ish score of 28 I tried to slap the off spinner all the way to the top of the Mound stand and got myself bowled meaning the fun had to stop. Walking back through the gate to a generous round of applause and some nice comments made it all worth while and afterwards I sat with my pads on the famous balcony taking it all in because tomorrow reality would kick back in and I'd be back with the children doing nets or fielding practice.

Still for the one day, I had got to play where millions of people from all over the cricketing world had dreamt of playing. For that one-day, we'd been able to feel like proper players and do the things that the best players get to do every day without thinking about it. For one day, I'd been able to tread in the same footsteps as some of the best the world has ever seen. No fairy tales, just a brilliant day.

46

MORE COMEBACKS THAN FRANK SINATRA

Most people didn't think I'd give up first team cricket and, if I was totally honest with myself, I probably didn't think I would either. At the outset, strange though it was, I managed to watch reasonably happily from the side lines but, if you have any sort of competitive edge about you, then you'll yearn to be a part of the top team and still like the attention that comes along with it. Sure it was nice to keep playing at a lower level and to be able to take a holiday with the family (and the academy took up a lot of my time) but, when Saturdays meant so much and had done for so many years, it was hard not to look over your shoulder at what you were missing, especially when you knew you were still more than capable of doing what you'd always done so well before.

I didn't miss the travelling and I certainly didn't miss some of the players but I missed seeing people and the gossip of the circuit and I absolutely missed some of the bollocks and the banter spoken in the dressing room. On top of all that the major problem was the huge gulf in standard between the first and second teams and so, when there was a problem and the 1st XI captain needed someone who could at least bowl straight, then they normally called on me, sometimes successfully, sometimes not. A couple of games here, a few there until half a season had gone by and I'm still getting the weekly enquiry about whether I'd return.

As I sat in the bath after losing the Sussex Cup Final at Horsham, with my right knee the size of a football, I vowed my time in the first team had finally come to an end and that I would turn out for the lower teams as I helped bring the young academy players through from the bottom upwards. That was the way it stayed until, after a fairly disappointing 2007, several key players left and some major holes needed filling. Stephen Greig, a good club stalwart, had returned to take the reins as first team skipper and quickly asked whether I'd come back as he needed someone who could hold an end up and keep it tight. That was now my role. No quick spells any more, no getting it through to the keeper chest high and, above all, no more bouncers or short pitched attacks, whether I liked it or not. They had long gone and you have to accept the new reality. You were now a veteran and it was only a matter of time before someone called you grandpa.

So 2008 gave me the chance to work on my fitness and prove to I could still play at a decent standard. Also the lure of reaching 400 first team league wickets was only 20-odd away and so back on the horse I jumped. The club had signed a South African lad called Matt Kleinfeld and, although we had several talented players, we struggled to get away from the lower reaches. The younger players failed to deliver and, despite the confidence of youth, the figures in the scorebook told a very different story. I was doing fine, doing what I was in the side to do and also getting a few handy runs as well, but staying away from the continual sniping in the bar was proving somewhat harder.

Halfway through the season, things changed when we picked up ex Sussex skipper Alan Wells who was available when his school duties allowed and his batting still showed plenty of class for a man nearing 50. He destroyed the premier fast bowler in the league at the time, Carl Simon for fun. He also had the best fielding arm which, for a bloke who jogged to get the ball and then bulleted it in from the boundary, was really quite obscene, certainly when compared with my now pop gun effort. Better still was the introduction of current Indian all-rounder Dinesh Mongia who came via the link with Lashings World XI. For some clubs this was a signing too far and argued he should not be allowed to play which, considering some of the overseas players that had played, was quite a demand. Some called it jealously, others thought it was against the spirit of the game and made a big fuss. If you look back at the history of the league, nearly every club could, at some stage, claim to have had a top drawer player in their side. For me, the argument was simple: if you want to play at the highest level then you have to do battle against the best around and get one over on them, otherwise what on earth are you doing there in the first place?

There was one match when dear old Dinesh, might not have got the spirit quite right. Playing against Brighton and Hove, he went on a one-man hitting spree standing there smashing it for four or six and, if it didn't go the distance, he just stood there in his crease resting on his bat handle refusing to take the single and then waited for the next ball to see if he could send it further into orbit. Which, on most occasions, he did. He finished around 180 not out and, despite it being great to watch, I'm not sure the MCC Spirit of Cricket DVD will tell you that what he did was in the best interests of the game. It was fair to say that tea was a slightly frosty affair between the sides and, when Brighton decided to block the crap out of it from ball one, you could tell it hadn't gone down well. Despite the dull finish, I managed to nip one back to get young Sussex academy player Tim Jarvis lbw for my personal milestone of 400 league wickets, a landmark I was proud to reach and which was, at the time I think, a league record. As they say, you can never take them away and, if and when someone betters it, which someone obviously will, they'll have to play for a long time and I guarantee they'll be pretty bruised and very knackered.

The season finished at the wrong time for us as we went unbeaten for well over half the campaign and, given a few more weeks, we would probably have won the league. I finished with a decent 30 wickets at around 14 a piece which, for an old bastard, was a good effort as well as getting three big wickets for 20 – Aravinda de Silva, Marvin Atapattu and Phil Simmons – in the annual Lashings match, so finishing up with Simmons bowled Simmonds had a nice ring to it. I could rightfully stick my fingers up at several people, but one thing I've learnt is that, if someone thinks one thing then it's unlikely you're going to change their mind. If you're a youngster and think the future is on your shoulders, then you see the older generation as passengers who need to head for the departure lounge. So, in the first match of the following season, that is exactly where I headed. You can usually tell you're not wanted when, during the off season, your name doesn't come up in conversation. You wonder whether you want to start the season or, even worse, fear you may not get picked which had never happened to me before. With the arrival of several new players, untried as they might be, you have a fair idea of what the captain or chairman has been telling them in order to get them to join. Some might be brilliant signings, others might not be so successful, but they all walk into the dressing room with that swagger you once had and, when that happens, it's normally time to slip away.

I realised my time was up after I only got to bowl four overs against Horsham on a wicket that suited me perfectly. I finished with one wicket for ten runs and the realisation that for the very last time in a game that could be considered as half decent, once and for all my time had run its course. I wished them all the best, with no hard feelings. It was my decision and I left with my head held high, knowing that if you've been a good player you'll always be a better player when you're not there to shatter that illusion. The simple truth was that, no matter how hard you try and deny it and how hard you fight against it, you simply can't outrun Anno Domini.

47

FINDING YOUR
HAPPY PLACE

There are some rare occasions when you stumble across a place where you fit in as soon as you arrive and wish you'd somehow managed to find it earlier. For me, Fonthill Lodge School was such a place. I'd been coaching youngsters in the area for what seemed like years, first for Sussex CCC, then as part of the academy and also at some of the best independent schools around like Christ's Hospital, Ardingly College, Reigate Grammar, Worth and Eastbourne College. As time went on, I started to feel I needed to be in one place so when a call came out of the blue from Jane Griffiths, head teacher at Fonthill, asking me whether I could teach PE, it seemed a good opportunity to simplify my frantic timetable.

The school was in good shape, partly because one nearby had closed due to falling attendances, and Fonthill had picked up nearly 40 children which had bolstered the finances and enabled them to hire a coach like me. To be fair, the standard of cricket was already pretty reasonable and we gave the other local prep schools a run for their money when it came to matches. The facilities may not have been as good as some of the other larger schools but it had a good reputation and this was 2005 when the economy was doing well and plenty of parents were happy to pay for private education with its smaller classes and, the time-honoured phrase, "value added".

I can't put my finger on exactly what was so special about the place but you felt it as soon as you walked through the doors. It was hard to explain and almost impossible to describe to prospective parents. Simply. the staff and, more importantly, the children were happy and that made for a thoroughly entertaining place. In reality, like most schools, it had a slightly mad cap existence that wouldn't have looked out of place in a TV mockumentary, such were the array of characters who worked there. Many, I'm sure, were nowhere near qualified enough to do the jobs they were being paid to do but everything seemed to come together successfully. While there was some serious talent on show, there were some who were truly hopeless and for them to be paid a salary was an affront to the jobs descriptions act. As there weren't many other male members of staff and as I could play at least two major sports properly, I came out smelling of roses. Getting paid to play five a side football is never the worst way to pay the mortgage. In fact, I played so much that my first touch improved to the extent it was miles better than it was when I actually tried to played football seriously.

As my workload increased, my role became a full time one, agreed over a handshake and, as they liked the positive PR that came with me running my cricket academy, they allowed me to combine the two roles when necessary. This also meant holiday pay and a pension and all things other people take for granted but for me were most welcome.

As the years passed, we decided to send Hannah and Lucy to Fonthill and they loved it just as much as I did. They would happily have gone to school seven days a week and, to be honest, I probably would have as well. It also gave me the chance to get to know some of the parents which had the advantage of extending my circle of friends but, as I was also on the staff, I did sometimes fear that some only wanted to talk to me so they could get all the school gossip. Many of the parents were delightful, while some were less so, but that's just part of life and the same the world over. One thing that did make things more difficult was the coming of email which would allow parents with a complaint to hide behind the keyboard to vent their frustrations. That is now part and parcel of teaching in the modern age but paying for your child's schooling does not make you an expert in educational matters. On the plus side, the children were great; children like Theo, part legend, part maniac, who made every single lesson an unforgettable experience. "So your brother can burp Happy Birthday, can he Theo? I was not aware of that, but thanks for letting me know." If you spent an hour with the likes of Theo and his mates, I defy you not to have a smile on your face by the end.

The financial crash of 2008 was the beginning of the end for Fonthill with an increasing number of parents unable to afford the fees. Year by year, the numbers would drop and the school's sports teams would get well beaten as there were fewer and fewer pupils to choose from – even Sir Alex Ferguson would have struggled to achieve much with the kids who remained. Sadly after months of speculation, gossip and talks behind closed doors, time was called in February 2011 when it was announced the school would close at the end of the summer term. Several factors were blamed for the school's failure – poor governance from the previous board, poor recruitment, poor investment decisions and an inability to compete in the ultra competitive private schools' market all played their part.

When the final assembly was over, I went to the privacy of my office, put my head in my hands and cried my eyes out. I was truly devastated that the ride was over, that I wouldn't be able to come to work to see my friends in the car park or in the staff room. To see the site sold off and all the years of history thrown into a host of skips was nothing short of disgraceful. I had been happier working there than I had been for years and saw it as a place I could not only coach sport but also get involved in other areas you never get to do as a freelance operator. Thankfully, Hannah had left a couple of years previously and Lucy was in the class that was due to be leaving anyway but both girls were distraught. It's never good to see your Dad cry. The majority of the children moved on happily enough and their parents move along with them, but the real losers were the staff who were cast aside and barely given more than a statutory handout for their years of effort and, in some cases, brilliant contributions.

As the years have passed, I look back at my time at Fonthill with immense pride and have to thank many people for helping me have such a great time there. Without doubt, though, the best thing to come out of it is my friendship with the delightful Mrs Clarke, who became my educational mentor, best mate and big sister all rolled into one as well as an occasional surrogate mother to our girls who hold her in the role of utter goddess. The staff room would have to be replaced by Starbucks and numerous other coffee shops in the years ahead as, unfortunately, the other option wasn't available any more. It's better to have loved and lost than never to have loved at all, I suppose . . .

48

END OF THE ROAD . . .
TWICE

After calling it a day with the first team in the opening week of the 2009 season, I was happily enjoying life in the thirds after deciding not to play for the seconds as they travelled just as much as the Ist XI. It meant I did not have to play every week and also could enjoy batting up the order. That was the plan, at any rate, but it quickly transpired that sadly things were never likely to work out and going from the Sussex Premier League the previous season to being asked to bat down at the bottom in the village league really was taking the piss. Not for the first time I wondered what game some people were watching but, in truth, it also signalled the beginning of the end of my time at East Grinstead.

The 2008 financial crisis was putting the squeeze on businesses up and down the country, including mine, and it became increasingly difficult to earn a salary from coaching. Despite the poor economic conditions, the senior management at East Grinstead Cricket Club felt there was still potential in putting on events such as the Lashings match and a celebrity evening and they decided to go ahead without the support of the cricket academy. One idea was to invite Geoff Miller, the former England spinner who was a superb speaker, and the Aussies, Dean Jones and Merv Hughes, for an Ashes evening in front of 400 people. Plans were put in place but, on the night there were, at most, 40 people in the audience, with the crowd probably outnumbered ten to one by the empty chairs. I doubt such a trio of well-known cricketing celebrities had ever performed in front of such a small crowd. Such a shame.

The other great shame was that this was the season where the fruit of the academy was starting to come through and it was a joy to see so many youngsters start playing in the men's sides. I suspect it was one of those things that was appreciated more by people outside the club than within.

As the winter of 2010 came and went and I continued to feel totally under-valued by the club, I wrote a long email to the new chairman telling him how I felt – and had done for a few years – and that it was time for me to move on. As my finger hovered over the keypad I knew that, once sent, that would be it. I wished everyone at the club all the best and prepared to depart. When I finally plucked up the courage and pressed send, it brought an end to my 14-year association with the club. It meant saying goodbye to a place where I had played much of my best cricket and where I had been an incredibly loyal servant and had enjoyed some happy and successful seasons. As soon as I'd sent the email, I felt a huge weight fall from my shoulders, akin to leaving a failing relationship. I had played, coached, worked, ran at least two busi-nesses from its premises and spent so many hours there that my car could find it on auto pilot. By 2010, however, it was nothing like the place I joined back in the mid-1990s. In had evolved into a huge money draining sports centre and further and further away from a cricket club. Over the years, many other good people had moved away feeling the same.

In truth, some would have been disappointed and some even shocked by my departure while I'm sure there would have been others who couldn't have given two hoots. For all the members who remembered the effort and loyalty as well as the wickets there would have been just as many who would have thought I was moving on because I couldn't compete anymore and wanted to play at a lower level where I could have a better chance at trying to be a hero every week. Nothing could have been further from the truth. I was devastated it had come to this and would have far rather stayed for the remainder of my playing days and then moved into various officer positions within the club. I had ambitions to be chairman and take the club on to higher things but that was not to be. When you don't feel you are wanted anymore, there's no point hanging around and so it was time to move on.

49

BACK WITH THE VILLAGE PEOPLE

When the place you've played at for years is effectively a sports centre and you can't get a drink in your own club because of yet another birthday party, wedding reception or private function then it starts to become almost laughable. Nearly the whole of the club had started drinking and socialising either in town or at the nearby tapas bar and we'd been doing it for years. As enjoyable as it was, it reminded me that a major part of any club was the social side and this had simply disappeared.

After leaving East Grinstead, I did have a few offers to stay in the Sussex League but they were never serious options as there was only one place I'd considered moving to and that was back to where it all started – Crawley Down. I'd promised a couple of old playing mates that I'd come back to play a season or two before I finished for good and I ended up playing for six, so at least I more than did what I said I would. If you make a promise, then you do your best to stick to it.

Even though the standard wasn't that special at times, the surroundings nowhere near as palatial and the approach to the matches different, the village scene still had plenty of charm. Teas were still splendid and it was only 26 steps from the dressing room to the bar so you'd be able to have a drink, talk to the opposition and sit on your stool discussing plenty of different topics until it was time to go home. For the first few months I still half-expected someone to tell me there was a party coming in and we'd have to move on elsewhere.

Another big advantage was that my parents lived nearby and, despite driving into the East Grinstead car park a couple of times by mistake on my way to the ground, it started to become more and more like home again as my focus shifted to the lesser lights of the Mid Sussex League and all the trivia that went with it. It also meant a return to plenty of places where I hadn't played for years and it was nice to catch up with a few old faces from my youth. Although I had to bite my lip and count to ten on more occasions than I care to remember, the pluses more than outweighed the negatives.

As a side, I'd coached quite a few of the players and, although I'm sure there were reservations about someone like me returning to play – someone used to a much higher standard and all the pitfalls and opinions that go with that – I think they enjoyed my contributions as I settled into the No 3 position which was a delight as I started to take my batting seriously and I could still bowl once the initial creeks and groans had worn off after a couple of overs. I started like a train with a century and a five-wicket haul against the reigning champions and never looked back. With the help of a more than decent Aussie called Warren Barker from Melbourne, who had married a local girl and lived in the village and some decent young players, we won far more than we lost. We were always in the top two before we ended up winning the league three years running and needed to move up to a better standard as far too many games were finishing before tea had even been laid out.

As with many things, one of the problems was trying to get players to believe in themselves and that they could perform at a higher level. With the pathways open from the Sussex Cricket Board and the league pyramid, there was no reason why the club couldn't reach at least Division Three of the County League before the size of ground and its restrictions would have become a problem. The club were put into division two of the West Sussex League and, despite some rude comments from some local rivals, we romped the league, going up as champions, the fourth year in a row we'd finished top of the pile. When we first did it, Jim Hewitt, a well-known personality at the club, had some fireworks left from the millennium which needed to be used before their sell-by date and so, after securing victory, what looked like a couple of nuclear warheads were carried into the ground and off they went to everyone's amusement. With every successive league title, the displays got bigger and better until, in 2015 when we spent far more on fireworks than we had on coaching, cricket balls and equipment combined, the display went on for well over half an hour and was quite superb. The end-of-year celebrations became legendary and it was also the place where my guitar came out on a regular basis, giving me the chance to practise one of my new passions and pretend I was Paul Weller or Bruce Springsteen, especially when I was too drunk to know the difference.

However, as 2016 saw me have yet another operation, this time on my heel, I'd begun to creek so much that I'd reached the stage that playing was not much fun and, with the increased travelling that came with moving leagues, I pretty well knew that, even though I was having a reasonable season with the bat, it was time to get out. I'd read before that the day you don't want to get out of bed on a Saturday, then you're virtually retired already.

I know a lot of people felt that, because I'd played for so long, I would never call it a day but no more than a couple of days after the last game of the season I knew I wouldn't be starting the following one in 2017. It had been nice to prove wrong a few people who said I couldn't bat for toffee as I averaged pretty well 50 over my six seasons back at Crawley Down, and I'm quite proud of that. It seemed the best place for me to finish as, more than 30 years earlier, it had been the place where it had all started.

For the first time since 1983, I wouldn't be looking at the fixtures and planning holidays around matches. My kit has remained in the garage all winter and I had no thoughts of having a hit in the nets or even a mental net in the kitchen. I always loved the smell of freshly cut grass because it meant summer was on its way, the weather was hopefully going to get better and, of course, it meant the cricket season wasn't too far away and, for me and for hundreds of thousands like me, that was just the best time of the year. I'm sure things won't be the same for a while but I'll just have to deal with it and quietly watch from a distance, wondering whether anyone will miss me or even notice that I'm not there anymore. To be honest, they probably won't. And why should they?

50

SO THIS IS WHAT HAPPENS ON SATURDAYS

Amazingly, the world still continued to turn on Saturday 6th May 2017. I had dreaded this day for many, many years and wondered how my meaningless life would revolve around the fact that for the first time since 1983, I wouldn't be starting the season like every other sensible person. What other things might you possibly want to do instead?

Unfortunately, this particular Saturday would have been a nonstarter anyway as I had attended a memorial service on the previous day down in Devon and so had stayed down to spend the weekend doing the sort of non-cricket activities that were to become the normal way of life. In a previous life, I'd have done everything I could have to have bombed back up the motorway in time for a 12.00pm start.

Within hours of the breakfast being cleared away, I was walking around a beautiful National Trust property wondering in which room the butler had done it, where he'd hidden the murder weapon and whether Miss Marple would pop out from behind the curtain to solve the crime before I ventured off for some lunch. All very pleasant but having little to do with winning the toss and bowling first on a damp one that should do plenty.

Over the next few weeks I managed to entertain myself by coaching at school on Saturdays, taking all sorts of teams to matches around the Sussex / Kent border and having the pleasure of discussing the world and its issues with some of the more palatable parents. Some matches were enjoyable and some were walkovers as the disparity between some schools became even more obvious than at first light. House matches were always the biggest chore, especially when they'd been organised so unbelievably badly and all the decent players ended upon the same team. Sometimes it was a bit like watching Manchester City play the Under 13's hoping for something other than a complete savaging.

Then there were the final matches of the football season hoping that West Ham wouldn't be sucked into the relegation mire after being fairly unimpressive all year. An absolute mauling by Liverpool hardly lifted the idea that not chasing a red ball around a field would have been the preferred option. A couple of pleasant lunches with Mrs Simmonds and friends rounded off the empty Saturdays without even attempting to swing a golf club or being taken shopping which was always my least favourite pastime in the summer.

It took three weeks before I received my first text message enquiring whether I fancied bringing my retirement to an early close. I'd been informed privately that I wouldn't be missed that much and there were plenty of able replacements ready to jump into my shoes. They certainly wouldn't be missing me for my fielding which had become so abject that I prayed the ball went nowhere near me for the whole forty-seven overs. With two wins out of the first three matches it seemed they might have a point, but after a stunning run which saw them bowled out for under a hundred week after week until the season finished it appeared that Crawley Down would lose convincingly whoever they put on the field and I was looking miles better than I probably was just by deciding to do something else instead. Not surprisingly, after such a run, they were relegated by August, which perversely is quite an achievement.

All this time, no matter where I was, like any hopeless addict, I needed my hourly fix of club cricket and this was maintained via the league websites and the up to date scorecards. Even if there were other activities to occupy me, I could quickly wander back to see that someone was 35 for 3 or that somebody else hadn't been able to field their third team. Come nine o' clock most of the results were in and I could peruse the various divisions to see who was excelling and how long my former side had managed to bat this week before being bowled out for around 70.

Towards the end of July, and with everyone else in my family overseas, I took up the invitation from a fairly desperate Fred Quirk and helped him out for his side Stonewall Park in one of the Kent leagues. Although the standard wasn't great, the blokes were excellent company and with a ground looked like something out of a Midsomer Murder episode. Set in the grounds of the Fleming Estate, they of the private banking family and related to Ian Fleming, the author of James Bond, the ground near Chiddingstone, looked out over the vast mansion and was for all money an absolute picture on a summer's day.

With such a picture perfect setting on offer, I thought it was only right to spoil the image by batting like a man who had picked up a bat since the previous August, which I hadn't. Your reputation always precedes you when making your debut for any team and they would have every right to wonder who on earth this bloke was and more importantly, how on earth he ever played at any decent standard. These days though, just by being willing enough to turn up and play you can make yourself invaluable.

Thankfully the opposition were so poor that two straight balls in three meant I walked away with my reputation slightly enhanced and the invitation for a return anytime I fancied. Tea was decent too which always helps. I played two or three more games when time allowed and by bowling at the stumps played a small part in keeping Stonewall in their division for another year. I was sure they wouldn't be missing me that much if I failed to materialise next April.

Time, they say heals most things and as the summer wore on, the season had passed by without too much drama and my return to the ranks of non-playing cricketer had been achieved. My biggest achievement was managing to avoid going shopping.

51

STUART, HE'S HERE

They say that you should never actually meet your heroes as it does nothing other than shatter your illusions and leave you feeling somewhat short changed. As a teenager, like most Hammers and red blooded males, I'd have given my right arm to have swapped places with striker Frank McAvennie who had the pleasant ability to score first division goals for fun, whilst drinking and shagging his way around London.

Back in the day, I would probably have been so star struck I'd have done nothing other than make some sort of mumbling sound to which he would have looked at me very strangely, thinking I needed some urgent therapy. However, the two times I have met him, I'd been hugely underwhelmed other than to realise that you might not have needed to have a crystal ball to see the problems that lay ahead for dear old Frank.

Surely it wouldn't be the same with the legendary David Gower. For the fact that I'd run across him three or four times and managed to maintain my dignity gave me the hope that if I did finally get to meet one of my all time heroes then I'd be able to behave properly. However, when I finally heard that he was probably coming to my book launch, then I'd be lying to say that I wasn't a little bit wobbly.

The fact that I actually having a book launch in itself was something that seemed a million miles away when I sat down and started jotting down my thoughts and memories a year previously. I'd spent many hours pondering the fact that I might be absolutely slaughtered for writing my story down in the shape of eighty-five thousand words. "I know he loves himself, but now he's written a book about himself" was all that was going around my head for many months as the chapters on the list slowly started getting ticked off until it was time to start letting various people start looking at my award winning words.

Over a very enjoyable lunch in London with Dan Evans, who'd helped edit the book and Derek Pringle, who wrote such a good piece for the foreword, we'd discussed my slight obsession with England's greatest ever left hander and the obvious fact occurred that as Derek knew him well from their playing and touring days, he'd be well placed for a bit of salacious gossip. What I wasn't expecting was for Derek to suggest that we invite him to the book launch.

Not for a single second did I expect him to attend, so I didn't take it terribly seriously as I ventured back to the shires of East Grinstead. However, when I received a call two weeks later to say there was every chance he would attend. I sat there quietly praying it would go well and mostly that he didn't think I was a nob.

Within days, I'd sent a couple of bottles of expensive wine to his address as a thank you and just as you'd expect, they weren't the sort of bottles that you could purchase at your local Majestic Wines. Pringle had foolishly given me his address to send them to and so I was now in possession of a vital piece of information if I fancied a casual piece of hero worship, which in most other languages actually comes under its proper heading, mild stalking.

As the big day arrived, the books had thankfully arrived in their masses, which was quite a sight when placed on your kitchen table. I had omitted the potential star attraction from public knowledge just in case something happened and he didn't pitch up, but more importantly so I wouldn't upset myself if that nightmare actually materialised.

The venue was a trendy bar in the city called Follys and as it was packed to the rafters on a Thursday just after payday, it did appear to most people that I had far more friends than was sadly the case. Situated at a quiet room on the ground floor, most of the guests, friends and family gathered more in wonderment at whether this book writing rumour was actually true, rather than for the offer of a few free drinks.

I'd been fixed on the entrance from the moment I'd arrived and then after forty years of hoping it still comes as something of a shock when your wife grabs you by the arm and tells you "bloody hell Stu, he's here!" Try to look like this thing happens all the time and whatever happens, don't fan girl him or do not start dribbling.

As I expected, he was eminently charming and delightful company. The look on people's faces when the saw that the book was genuine and had a cover and everything was pleasing, but nothing compared to when they saw who'd just arrived. Not only was it my book launch but the fact that a national treasure has just walked in seemed to wash away all the worries I'd had over its reception since the day I opened my laptop and started tapping away. Additionally the look on my Dad's face when he saw who I was talking to was worth all the effort alone.

As the drink flowed, the cameras snapped away catching the moment for prosperity and as is the way nowadays, social media went into overdrive. Better still, my new bestie David had a good cackle at my speech which seemed to go down a treat and my only regret was forgetting to do a good gag I'd thought up in the car at the expense of Kevin Spacey who'd run into a spot of bother the day before. Never mind.

Selfies, autographs and back slapping passed along as hundreds of books were signed and sold before it was time for the fun to stop as the last trains had to be caught. The guest of honour was amiable and friendly, took more photos than was humanly possible whilst answering everyone's questions despite how much some people had consumed. The signed copy of my own book and the message he left will now be placed in the never to be sold box.

The following day, after the photos had gone on Facebook and Instagram (to which I had only joined the previous morning) meant the expected buzz continued for a few hours until life returned to normal, as it was always going to.

I can obviously understand those who say you should never meet your idol, but tonight I was nothing other than hugely impressed with Mr D I Gower. Sometimes its good to finally meet your hero after years of waiting and wondering. I hope he enjoyed the wine.

52

TIME TO GET BACK ON THE HORSE SON

There are certain people you meet in life who it's extremely dangerous to go to lunch with. David Bowden is definitely one who fits into that category.

For those who haven't had the pleasure of meeting him, David had a very successful career in business and has spent the majority of his retirement in various positions helping Sussex CCC from sensible sounding board to President of the club. He was also heavily involved in the setting up and then the administration of the Spen Cama trust, after his amazing legacy left millions to both Sussex as well as his club, Preston Nomads. To be honest, if I started listing the things he's done to try and better the fortunes of cricket in the county, then I'd probably need another chapter altogether.

I'd got to know David well over the last few years and was always happy to chat over the things that crossed our minds. He

241

is one of those priceless individuals who have the ability to make you feel good about yourself even though at times I wondered if I was actually any good at the things we'd talked about in the first place. So when I was invited out to lunch in Hove, as means of an apology for him not being able to attend my book launch in London, I was more than happy to attend.

What I hadn't bargained for was that by the time that the bill was settled, I'd be back involved at the county for the first time in over ten years as Vice President of the Cricket Foundation, the new independent chairman of the Crawley hub of clubs, sitting in various meetings in the board room at Hove and worst of all, been persuaded to come out of retirement to play for the Sussex over 50's. For the cost of a nice juicy steak and some chips I hope he thought he'd got a good deal.

After finishing coaching as a job the previous July, it was probably just what I needed to get me used to not going into various schools for the first time sine 1991. So far I've very much enjoyed trying to help the charity as well as attempting to get more children playing cricket at schools and clubs, which in today's mobile dominated world is a much harder task than it used to be.

However, of all the thing I'd agreed to sign up to, getting back on the horse and starting to play again left me with the most knots in my stomach. I'd done a reasonable job getting through the dreaded first year of not missing Saturdays too much, but this meant starting to take it fairly seriously again.

To my immense surprise, Jacky, Hannah and Lucy were really behind the idea and actively encouraged me to get the kit out of the garage and dust it all off. With matches on a Wednesday until you reached the knock out stages, it wouldn't affect my weekends and to be honest a bit of exercise wouldn't have gone amiss in terms of the expanding waistline and declining fitness levels.

The obvious downsides were that there was a reason we'd all

stopped playing and that was because we'd all got old, we'd all had way too many injuries to carry and most of all whether we wanted to admit it to ourselves or not, nowadays we were all crap.

The upside however was far more beneficial. It was delightful to catch up with a load of people who I hadn't seen for years and after attending the first set of nets at the beautiful Arundel Castle, it was like you'd never been away. I'd been able to catch up with the likes of the legendary Andy Meads and I was particularly thrilled to see Richard Seagar who'd I'd played with at Lewes Priory and who'd been an unbelievable help in my younger years. The instant abuse that I received for not going that grey reminded me of how much I'd missed the banter of the dressing room. Additionally, everyone in that dressing room could actually remember The Jam or Simple Minds in their pomp, which was a bonus rather than my former team mates looking at me as if I was some sort of fossil.

Generally, most things seemed to still work as I listened to tales of the new county championship and how seeing as nobody has any pace to work with any more it was a very different game to the one which you'd been playing for the last forty years. Generally speaking, it was just the admission to yourself, that even though you refused to acknowledge it, you were now over fifty and still unbelievably stiff. The rest was up to you in terms of how you dealt with that age related dilemma.

Once the season approached, the nets increased as did the reappearance of old team mates and some older opponents. Once you'd hit the bar, the themes were all the same as you discussed games, players and the time old question of what had happened to the fortunes of so many of our mates from the good old days of the Sussex County league and the ones fortunate enough to make it through to the pro ranks.

Of all the things that were discussed, there was now a communal honesty when it came to the characters and stars of yesteryear. People could now be brutally honest about who were the best, worst, as well as the most over and under rated people on the circuit. It was generally refreshing after nearly two decades I could finally admit publically what I'd only divulged to one or two people and that was that we'd all been hopelessly jealous of the major teams in the league. With their greater pool of players, better attended training sessions and the obvious ability to turn up every week knowing there was a fair chance they'd win. Add in the fact that you'd be challenging for silverware every season and the occasional win down at the seaside and taking the big sides on single handed didn't seem quite so palatable.

The new fixture list also took me back to proper grounds that I'd not visited in years and the realisation that despite there being plenty of charm in the return to village cricket, you'd also been playing at some fairly dreadful places over the last few years.

With the fact that the ECB and Sport England have been promoting over age sport and participation, Sussex CCC had done their bit to encourage extra number returning to the sport and I was amazed at how many sides the county ran. Two over 50's, four over 60's and apparently some of the over 70's were quite a force to be reckoned with. If you listened to some of the old sages, we all had another twenty-five years of chasing a red ball around a field. Thankfully, the free clothing that we'd managed to blag from Keith Greenfield at Hove meant we at least looked the part. I didn't have the heart to admit that getting the XL training top on was become quite an effort but I'm certain that most of my team mates noticed. My children certainly did.

The Sussex first team was made up mostly of players who'd played some form of county cricket in their youth as well as a few who had played for sides at first and second team level in the

1980's and 90's. The dressing room resembled a war room prior to going out to field with the sight of more bandages, strappings and neoprene fused in with the smell of various ointments for eleven ageing men attempting to stretch off the years of self inflicted physical abuse. Paul Brooks wore so much neoprene that he might as well gone out to bowl in a wetsuit, which it has to be said he did very well. As for Michael Bell, the ex Warwickshire and Surrey seamer, he was about the only player who could have been accused of being a ringer as he could annoyingly still pass for being thirty-five and played like the former pro he was. He was an incredibly nice bloke as well, which made it all the more annoying. As far as I was concerned, I might occasionally be able to pass for someone under the dreaded age of fifty but even if I was, I bowled so poorly that most of the oppositions wouldn't have cared less either way. They just lined up the forty-two mile an hour thunderbolts that I was offering up with relative glee and sent it back from where it came.

Middlesex at the delightful Blackstone Academy were the first opponents and they were swiftly set aside. I managed to recover from bowling a flat one first ball to take a few wickets for not many as we bowled them out for around 150. Unbeknown to me at the time, it would be my best effort by a country mile. Messers Stratton, Pannett and Robinson made very light work of the total and all in all we patted ourselves on the back for starting well and looking like like a decent side.

However, two weeks later, those congratulations had disappeared after we lost two games to Essex and Kent that we should never have and our chances of making the knock out stages had declined alarmingly. I'd managed to snap in both games and started to resemble the stiffest man in the whole of Sussex. After winning at Buckinghamshire, we were duly thrashed by Berkshire and qualification was now out of our hands.

Despite hammering Surrey at Eastbourne, I had now come to the conclusion after a woeful three over spell that the stiffness couldn't continue. I'd started to slip into the pathetic bracket and was generally embarrassed. I needed something different and received some good natured advice on how yoga and pilates might now help my general lack of movement in a vain attempt to stop looking like a cardboard cut out who could barely land it in the right place.

On World Cup semi final day, we beat a woeful Herts side by ten wickets with myself and Scott Stratton getting the total of 100 in just over ten overs. After a couple of useful lower order knocks I think one or two people thought I might as well have a go at seeing if my batting wasn't as bad as my bowling had become. Thankfully, out of nowhere, Berkshire had lost and we'd managed to burgle our way into the knock out stages on run rate.

In the quarter-finals, however, we lost a tight game to Suffolk during the hottest spell that we'd witnessed in the UK for many years and that, as they say was that. There would be no end of season matches and we all went back home up the A13 licking our wounds, wondering whether it would be worth reappearing next year. The good news was that two of our best players, Scott Stratton and Jason Robinson had been selected to play in the inaugural over 50's World Cup in Sydney with the obligatory England blazer and playing shirt thrown in for good measure. Not that any of us were the least bit jealous of them going off to Australia to represent their country whilst it had started to get freezing back home.

Amazingly, my offer to go out there to help carry the drinks and towels never did get a response. Next time perhaps.

53

FINALLY TIME TO SAY THANK YOU

My parents probably installed in me the need to always say thank you when it was time to say my farewells and I suppose this is no different, only potentially somewhat longer.

I'd like to start by thanking Daniel Evans for editing and proof reading my words. It does help when your mate used to be the sports editor of a national Sunday newspaper, but he's encouraged me from the beginning of the project and thankfully for my pride and my sanity, he's not changed too much around. I'd also like to thank Fred Quirk for providing another set of eyes over the thousands of words on offer and for pretending to enjoy the experience.

To Derek Pringle, who has been kind enough to write the foreword. It's a privilege to have someone of Derek's calibre both as a player and a journalist and I was obviously thrilled and delighted when he agreed to do so.

To David Bowden, for writing a lovely piece for the updated version, telling me off for swearing and most importantly for persuading me to return to one of the things I love the most.

To Bill Greenhead, many thanks for the superb artwork and sketches that you have done for the front and back covers. You really are a very talented man.

To all my team mates, work mates and coaches along the way both past and present, a massive thank you for everything that you've done for me over the years. Without you it wouldn't have been anywhere near as much fun.

To Janet and Malcolm and the rest of my family for always being there for me when I needed them most.

To Hannah and Lucy, thank you so much for encouraging me to start, continue and then finish this project. I am hugely proud of many of the things I've done in my life, but nothing compares with how immensely proud I am of you two.

However, my biggest thanks goes out to Jacky, who has stood by me and had my back for so many years now. I know that I wouldn't have got anywhere without her help and support as well as her love and guidance. As her career continues to reach the stratospheric level it has to this present day, she has still encouraged me to continue to do the things I love and to still chase my dreams. I have been lucky enough to meet some truly incredible people over the years, but she is quite simply the most remarkable person I have ever met in my entire life.

Finally to Richie, David, Trevor, Scott and Virgil, James, Allan and one or two others that rarely get a mention, thank you so much for popping up throughout the years and allowing me the chance of dreaming that one day I could be like one of my heroes. You see for me, the chance to dream and have an imagination is as great a gift as anyone can bestow upon anybody and it should never, ever be crushed or hidden away for all to see. Would anyone ever have wanted to be me, I very much doubt it. However if they had done, I hope they would have had as nice a time as I've had along the way.

Ramblings No. 1
BIG MATCH DAY

It's the time when you really do wish you'd been able to hit the very highest heights. Walking into Lord's on a major match day is the one time when most people coming through the turnstiles wish they'd had the ability and the luck to be able to perform in front of a packed house on the biggest stage at the most famous cricket ground in the world. The crowds arrive hoping their favourite players will produce something special that will be more than worth the price of the tickets. It is a ritual that has gone on for decades and will continue long past the time when we've all put our cues back in the rack and gone upstairs to see what the fuss was really all about.

The fact that I'm here at Lord's on May Bank Holiday in 2017 is something of a sore point. I was meant to be in New York but, after British Airways cancelled all its fights because of some sort of cyber attack, I didn't even get past the terminal gates at Heathrow. So, on Sunday morning, instead of walking around Central Park, I got to walk down East Grinstead high street which, I know, doesn't have quite the same appeal. The slight compensation for me was that I was now able to get my little red MCC passbook and go to Lord's to see the ODI between England and South Africa the following day.

Getting up to catch the train to London is not one of my favourite things and, to make matters worse, I realise to my horror I look like I've got dressed in the dark but have no time to alter my fashion faux pas as I'll miss the 08.37. I look like a poor man's college lecturer and have managed to pull off the worst combination of jacket, chinos and shoe selection known to man. For someone who spends most of the summer in trainers or flip flops, having to put a tie and jacket can seem like a chore made worse when I dress so badly. When I bump into a friend at the station and see his reaction I know my wardrobe choices will haunt me all day – and so they should.

As the queues thin towards the entry gates, the expectations on the faces of both adults and children are a joy to see. For those entering for the first time, Lord's really is a place of beauty and a theatre where only the lucky few can perform. For the youngsters, you hope they will be able to attend for many years to come, able to see some of the geniuses on show. On my first trip, way back in 1979, I got to see Gower and Botham, Greenidge and, of course, Vivian Richards while today's generation are able to see Root and Stokes, Hashim Amla and the brilliant AB de Villiers, on what might be his final appearance at the home of cricket. Such players are worth the admission money alone and today is the day you are going to watch the match on your own terms and, most importantly, through your own eyes. Too many times we are bombarded with opinions and statistics by journalists and especially TV commentators, all trying to get across their point of view. As we know, some are better than others but there is something particularly appealing about being able to see the whole match unfold in front of your own eyes. To be able to work out what's going on and seeing it all in the widest possible vision rather than on four square TV walls is something special.

A day at Lord's will give me the chance to bump into plenty of old friends from the circuits I used to patrol and this year, for the first time, I will be giving a different reply when they ask me if I'm still playing. It's five weeks into the season and it still feels strange not to be walking out of the door on a Saturday to go and try my luck at some ground or other. Even not being there to see the elite players warm up hasn't made me miss that part of playing too much. I think I stopped warming up before a match around ten years ago.

With South Africa winning the toss and with the wicket looking pretty green, it is no surprise Mr de Villiers asks England to bat and that quickly looks like a good decision. England have already won the ODI series so have decided to rest four regular players including Ben Stokes, which is a major disappointment for the whole crowd and especially the younger watchers as he has become a proper box office player. Even a middle-aged git like me is gutted. It matters as England start to bat like the bunch of hopeless tossers they can sometimes be. Jason Roy goes first with yet another nick to first slip, gone for four in the first over. The crappy start gets worse as Joe Root, the one player I really wanted to watch and get a big score, decides to personally let me down by playing all around one and is lbw for two. He's a great player and apparently a lovely bloke but today, for the next five minutes, he's going to have to sit on the naughty step until I forgive him. It gets worse as Eoin Morgan nicks off for bugger all and England are right in the mire. Getting worse still as, just for a change, first ball next over, Alex Hales plays one of his famous flat-footed prods and nicks to the slips to make it 16 for four. His personal contribution today at the home of cricket is a stunning effort of one run.

Have none of these players had the decency to realise I'm still hugely pissed off that I'm not in New York? You would think they could try to cheer me up by at least trying to bat properly. I know it's a bit green and doing a little bit off the pitch, but will they please shape up and not ruin what has already been a shitty weekend. It's at times like this that you don't want to hear the ex-England captains on Sky TV try and give a sensible explanation for what's happening in case they upset the players so much that they never get another interview out of them again. Please say it as it is, we've all been 16 for four at some time in our playing days so let's not beat around the bush and say what every punter is saying all around the ground – that England are batting like a bunch of clowns on the village green. Come on Athers, Nasser and Bumble! What's the worst that could happen? You'll only lose you're highly lucrative jobs – nothing too serious. . .

Jos Buttler is in and he's the new type of hero. Kids love him, fighting fire with fire and taking the positive approach to get his country back into the game. Well not today as he also nicks off for a brilliantly made four to leave England 20 for five. After less than six overs Adil Rashid walks through the gates and onto the hallowed turf. He can hold a bat, but batting at number seven for England is surely way too high, says the crowd to each other. But what do they know because 99.9 per cent of them haven't played first class cricket and don't have an opinion worth worrying about. Well, I'm afraid they do have an opinion and sometimes, to the horror of the olds boys' club that is professional cricket, a lot of them do know what they are talking about because they are the ones who spend time watching, playing and studying the game. They might not have been in the inner sanctum of the first-class dressing room and they might not speak the same language as some of the players on the circuit, but they know a good player, know a poor shot and know a strange left field selection when it walks through the pavilion gates. Rashid is caught at second slip first ball after a dreadful flash at a wide one and England are 20 for six.

Thirty thousand spectators can't all be wrong. This is pitiful and most will have paid around £100 to have the pleasure of watching it happen in front of their own eyes. For some of the fine folk, the horror of the game being over before the picnic hampers come out and the champagne corks are popped is now a real possibility and that just won't do. It's all very well to repeat the well-used line of "it's the way I play and you have to take the rough with the smooth" but surely there needs to be some sense of judging the situation and not flashing your bat at every wide delivery that comes your way when your team is deep in the shit. It might be the modern way to play but sometimes, like today, that theory appears to be utter bollocks.

For Jonny Bairstow, this is now the chance to impress the selectors and stake a claim for a starting spot in the Champions Trophy line up. The ironic roar of approval from the crowd when he plays a sensible shot that doesn't involve anyone getting out is both amusing and laughable at the same time. For the South Africans, the sight of the once fearsome Morne Morkel is a reminder that, no matter how good you once were, fast bowling is a back breaking job and at the age of 33 he looks like the man who is well down on pace after recovering from another injury. As Bairstow and David Willey patiently start to rebuild the innings, and with the debutant Toby Roland-Jones looking impressive later on, England manage to bring some sanity back into the game. Bairstow is now without doubt a top-drawer player and has proved many critics wrong in the way he has scored mountains of runs all over the world. Today, both he and Willey play shots of the highest quality but, after such a poor start, it's only a matter of time before the innings comes to an end for a paltry 153. As the crowds make their way to meet friends and get stuck into their lunches, it's hard not to be mightily pissed off with what has just happened.

The South African innings is far more positive and they make a mockery of England's hopelessly low score. I'm sure David Willey isn't doing it on purpose but someone needs to tell him that Hashim Amla has scored around 6999 of his 7000 ODI runs off his legs, so it might be a good idea not to bowl anywhere near leg stump. It's just a theory but not one that the England opening bowler seems to be following, much to the derision and groans of the full house as the South African run machine and bearded wonder takes advantage of the continual offerings on his pads.

It's the mid-afternoon lull that causes most problems, trying not to fall asleep with your mouth open only to be caught by the cameras. As the game meanders, you start to think of ways to amuse yourself; you try your hand at being a Test Match Special commentator for a few overs seeing if you can actually talk to yourself for that long without impersonating Henry Blofeld. It's harder than you think. The talk around the Members' bar is that John Noakes, the former Blue Peter presenter, has died and if you had a pound for every time someone said "Get Down Shep", then you'd have had enough money to buy one of the rather overpriced beef rolls on offer at the bar. It's also a rollover on the Euro lottery and so many people are talking about what to do with their winnings once they scoop the jackpot of £121 million. How many will actually have bought a ticket ?

However, the best sight of the day is the chance to watch AB de Villiers come out to bat. With the match sure to end in victory for his side, the stands are half empty when, as his name is announced across the ground, people dash back from the bars and, within a few minutes, almost every seat in the house is taken. There may be many ways to judge who has been the greatest of all time, and it's simply an unanswerable question, but there are some players who can make people put down their drinks, stop talking to their friends at the bar or over lunch and go back to their seat and watch as a genius has just walked onto the pitch. AB de Villiers is such a player. The man goes through the gears until he decides he has had enough and the time has come for him to tear into the England bowlers who disappear all over the Lord's outfield, finally bringing proceedings to a close much earlier than most people had thought at 11am.

It wasn't the match I had hoped to watch but being at Lord's was still special. If a big blue genie ever did grant me three wishes, there would be a quite a few things on the list. Hat trick for West Ham against Chelsea or Spurs, rock god at Wembley Stadium, you know the sort of thing. But to score a brilliant hundred for England at Lord's and then walk off slowly to a standing ovation in front of a packed house would be right up there. Along with having that winning Euro lottery ticket, of course.

Ramblings No. 2

FAME AND THE GREEN-EYED MONSTER

I had arrived in Melbourne on the premise of doing some work for a travel company just in time for the opening match of the Cricket World Cup in February 2015. After checking in at The Langham, the swanky hotel in the centre of town, I discovered my fellow guests included players from England and Australia. Also booked in over the next few days were players from India and South Africa. By a stroke of luck, I'm in a position to see some of the most famous people in the sport, a couple of whom are simply world famous. I've always been fascinated by the notion of fame and the effects it has. What makes someone more famous than somebody else? Who chases fame and what they perceive as the trappings of success? If you'd like fame yourself, what would you be prepared to do to get it? And what level of intrusion would you be prepared to put up with? For the next six days in Melbourne, I would have a front row seat for all the above.

As I ventured down on the Saturday morning, I was at the breakfast buffet, looking for ketchup of all things, when I realised I'm standing in front of Shane Warne and Australian captain Michael Clarke. Even in my jet-lagged state, I tried my best not to look too star struck. As I smiled at one of the most famous people I've ever met, Shane Warne looked at me and said: "Mate, you've either had a hell of a night or you've only just landed in Australia." Now I was free to have a little chat and, even though I was still half asleep, they both seemed very personable and our chat lasted for about two minutes at best. That's it, just two minutes. 120 seconds. We wished each other well, I made a small joke about hoping Michael Clarke had a terrible day as England win, we all laughed politely and I headed back to my table in order the attack the sausages.

Now the strange thing is that, for Mr Warne and Mr Clarke, those two minutes will pass off just as simply as it would for me chatting to someone in the supermarket queue. They will never, ever remember meeting me in the breakfast bar but I will remember it for the rest of my life – it's as simple as that. My 120 seconds with probably the greatest bowler of all time. Michael Clarke is extraordinarily talented and had a fantastic career but, from the moment he started seeing Liz Hurley, Shane Warne passed from cricketing royalty into the world of outright world fame. So why is he so famous? He's a leg spinner, that's all. The thing is he consistently bowled a leg spinner better than anyone before him and, added to his personality and attitude, he became someone people will talk about until the day he dies, and beyond. Some people have one amazing skill and not much else, but that one skill is enough to open up a whole new world, a world where no one can really comprehend what the level of scrutiny must be like for someone who hasn't really chased fame. It's simply found him as he has a talent that only one person a generation is lucky enough to have. To live such a life must be bizarre in the extreme and I'm sure there are many days when he and others like him wish they could have their old life back and return to being just a face in the crowd.

The central question is whether people who have fame thrust upon them, so to speak, are aware of price they may end up paying. Yes, they have their lucrative endorsements and sponsorship deals and appear in TV shows and in newspaper and magazine articles but does that give other people the right to march up to them and demand an opinion? Are they, in truth, making a deal with the devil with their privacy becoming the main price of fame? It is that strange notion about fame that some people feel they have the right to pass judgment on a person they really don't know at all.

That same morning as I was preparing to go into Melbourne, I watched as one England fan came into a hotel he wasn't even staying at and abused Mitchell Johnson while he was waiting for a taxi. He just stood in front of Johnson and told him at full blast he thought he was "f***ing useless" and that "he couldn't bowl for shit". Now I know it takes all sorts to make up the world, but I was utterly embarrassed to be English at that moment. Johnson bowled at the speed of light the previous winter and destroyed England as they were thrashed out of sight. He's one of the best sportsmen in the world, good looking, and is rich beyond most people's imagination yet a fat, balding, middle aged bloke from Barnsley has decided to come all of the way to the hotel to tell Mitchell Johnson he thinks he's shit. He probably thought he was trying to get under Johnson's skin before the big match and give England a cunning advantage, but the man was a complete arse. Does the price of admission allow you to hunt someone down and abuse them to their face? Surely nothing gives you the right to behave like that. When I asked Johnson whether this sort of thing happened much, he said: "More than most people realise. Everyone thinks they know me just because they recognise me from the TV and that gives them the right to have an opinion."

When it was time for the players to depart for another city and another match, the Indians and South Africans came to take their place and their demeanours could have been more different. Now I had known the South African head coach Russell Domingo for more than 20 years since our time together in Port Elizabeth. We are good mates and he's a great guy who has done bloody well for himself. His players in the South African side were well-mannered and polite and, even though some were true international stars, they were humble and you couldn't help but like them. AB de Villiers and Dale Steyn might be judged two of the biggest stars on the cricketing planet but they were down to earth and pleasant. They walked around Melbourne without a care, signing autographs and taking selfies without thinking too much about it. When I saw them the next morning, they all stopped for a quick chat, not because I was Russell's mate, but because they were decent guys.

In sharp contrast, the Indian players walked around the hotel with their entourages, including business managers and agents. I guess it's just how they live their lives on a daily basis as they are treated like film stars in their own continent. The tables weren't big enough to squeeze everyone around as so many people had an interest in the players. Throw in the huge Indian press corps and things really did become unmanageable. If you did catch their eye they smiled but the amount of time that someone like Virat Kohli gets on his own must be minimal. They might be gods in their own land but I'm sure the pressures that come with it are unbelievable. Not rude, not disrespectful, just a completely different way of having to live your life when all the extras are thrown in.

Sometimes, the strangest thing is to see how people you know react when they come into contact with someone they perceive as famous. Some are disappointed when they meet their heroes because they expect them to be more like they appear in the glossy magazines when, in reality, they are normal people being themselves. Others fall into the trap of becoming complete name droppers, believing the associated stardust will somehow make their lives more appealing while another group are more old fashioned, believing that to be famous you need some sort of talent to begin with, be it something like an actor, musician or a sporting star. This makes the new-found wannabe celebrity of the reality television and internet age even harder to understand, especially if they are coining it all along.

Of all the famous people I have ever met, the most bizarre meeting was when I took a football team from Lingfield Notre Dame – now called Lingfield College – in Surrey to play a match in Regents Park in London. We were hopelessly late and had a get a move on so not to miss kick off. As I ran with spare footballs, water bottles and first aid kits, I passed a man who looked vaguely familiar but, as I was in such a rush, I barely turned around. I did notice he was more handsome than a normal bloke should be, but it was raining hard and he was wearing one of those huge Australian wax jackets and had a hat on, so it was hard to see him clearly. He doesn't half look like David Beckham, I thought to myself, and moved on, thinking there could be worse people to look like. Then, out of curiosity, I turned and saw the tattoo on the back of his neck . . .. Bloody hell, that IS David Beckham!

As I went to introduce myself to the opposition coach, I had to sign the team sheet and noticed that, among a long list of foreign and mostly Russian names, the one that stood out was Brooklyn Beckham. Normal sort of stuff you get at a school match where arguably the world's most recognisable superstar was going to be watching from the touch line. He's only got 115 England caps and played for the biggest clubs in the world, so I'm sure he'll appreciate my cutting-edge tactical knowhow from the side of the pitch. He might have made his name by scoring from the half way line once but I'd scored an absolutely world class goal from 25 yards against the Under 12s a few weeks earlier so I had no worries.

The match might not have been a classic but most people wouldn't have noticed for most of the spectators were looking at the celebrity with the high-pitched voice passing instructions onto his son. As half time came, most of my team hadn't realised who our guest on the touchline was until they came in for my inspirational chat when, not for the first time, they didn't pay the slightest bit of attention to the fact that we were losing and started asking if they could take a few selfies. It was then that my competitive instinct took over and I told them I wanted to get back on the bus with a win and a place in the next round of the cup. I also told them, in a voice just loud enough so David might hear, that he was a father and there to watch his boy play football without being hassled. It worked a treat as the man himself came over and thanked me for what I'd said. Amazingly, he told me he normally has to leave matches after about five minutes because he is swamped by children and adults alike, which is a shame.

The second half was an equally poor affair, apart from the perfect ball-come-man tackle on young Brooklyn by our own Sam Firminger, who was such a top lad that he's welcome at our house anytime he likes. It was such an awesome challenge I thought Beckham Jnr was going to end up in the trees. We lost 3-1 to a side we should have beaten, Mr Beckham wished us all well for the rest of the season and the lads were thrilled. We only had a brief conversation but he seemed like a decent bloke, albeit far too handsome for his own good. I decided not to ask him where Victoria was and thought better of telling him the tattoo on his neck was not one of his better ideas. I'm sure he'll survive without my opinions.

The moral of this story is in what happened afterwards as we headed back through rush hour London. As you might imagine, the lads were thrilled to have seen David Beckham and their social media went into overdrive. For my part, I texted my daughters to tell them what had happened and so, when we arrived back at the school, we were greeted by parents wanting to know if their children were making stuff up again. When I got home, I was greeted by two children sprinting down the stairs as if I'd just returned from a six-month tour of Iraq. They wanted to know everything and whether I had mentioned their names to Mr Beckham and whether he knew of their existence. They had plastered the news all over Facebook and so friends from all over the world knew what I'd done at work that afternoon. My phone rang with friends enquiring about what had actually taken place the previous day, whilst I even had two calls from the local press checking if it was a genuine story.

The story just snowballed, as somehow Chinese whispers took over and brought a whole new side to what had actually happened. Suddenly the match was now played at the school fields at home and not in Regents Park and as many as four different age groups had taken part with everyone's sons playing. There were even several mothers who somehow found a paparazzi photo of Beckham in the rain and stuck it on their Facebook page and made out he'd been watching a match at Lingfield Notre Dame. These were bright, hard working women who were not interested in the actual facts but had been caught up in all the excitement. Forget Chinese whispers, this was turning into something out of Walter Mitty.

The stories and gossip carried for a couple of days until, thankfully, sanity returned and you could sit back and realise all this had been created by the fact that one very famous man had put on his coat in the rain and gone to watch his lad play football. No more, no less. Should the fact that he is one of the most recognisable faces on the planet make any difference? Well it seems it did, if only to make other people's lives seem that little bit more exciting for a day or two.

Ramblings No. 3
INTO THE NEXT LIFE

They say that a lifestyle is a terrible thing to waste. One day
towards the start of the 1999 campaign, I sat in a crowded
dressing room after a pre season friendly between Sussex and
Surrey had been curtailed due to the heavens opening, giving
everyone a break from whatever they were doing, myself included
as I'd been there lobbing my assortment of pies at expectant bat-
ters in the nets whilst the game was going on.

As the subject turned to what a couple of recently retired players had set up in London, it dawned on me that it was a topic that
was never far away from anyone who has such a potentially short
career span. Its also one that can turn suddenly with an injury or
worst of all a loss of form so great that your livelihood takes a
turn for the worse and its off to the recruitment consultants
for you. As the season draws towards its close the subjects
becomes more talked about as many fear that the worst is about
to happen. Whether they like it or not and even though it's the
first answer that most will fall back upon when the axe does fall,

not everybody can go into coaching as there are simply not enough jobs to go around. That's without forgetting that just because you were once a player, it will automatically make you a great coach, I'm afraid that's one of the biggest misconceptions going.

For the players who are lucky enough to get paid to play their chosen sport for a living, not that many are smart enough to see that the end is inevitable and have started planning for it, because as night follows day, there will be a time when the fun has to stop. Many delude themselves that they have something still to offer whilst the ones who have the luxury to leave on their own terms are few and far between. Like it or not most players get sacked, some more than once and its only a tiny handful that a lucky enough to end up in the media or the TV studio.

The trouble is that it is their profession that defines them as a person. They are a professional athlete with all the supposed sexiness and the allure that comes along with it. You're not John Smith the financial planner, or John Smith the butcher, baker or candle stick maker. You're John Smith the pro sportsman. When people meet them and find out what they do they immediately pick up their ears and take notice, which when you consider how short some player's careers are it is quite a thing to hang on to. For someone who will now have to work for around fifty years, the fact that one tenth of it was spent as a professional cricketer will still be the thing that you will want to probably be remembered for, not being a teacher or an accountant which might take up the the rest of your years of gainful employment. Added to the common misconception that because you've been a professional, you will have automatically earned a small fortune from your playing days and therefore won't really have to worry about where the next meal is coming from, the sympathy vote won't be that overwhelming. The players never seem to have the heart to tell those enquiring that they've probably been earning relative peanuts, because no one wants to take away the supposed glamour of what they have been doing for the last few years. There are very few millionaire players out there, most will have earned a fraction of what the household names should have and almost all of the players will have been on much less than people would realise. The sad part is that many of them still have aspirations of living life with champagne tastes whilst sadly on beer money.

So what does one do when the rug is pulled from under your feet and you no longer feel you can walk into the dressing room to soak up the gossip and talk bollocks to your mates. The sponsored car has been returned and there's no more free stash to nick and sell to the players at your club. You're now an outsider who has been forced to re join the rest of society and this for some can lead to the mother of all mid life crises, many going on for years. For some the end of their careers is like having all your limbs amputated and then sown back incorrectly and having to watch as everything turns from sugar to crap fairly quickly.

The problem that awaits most ex players is that it takes them quite some time to realise that they are spectacularly under qualified to do most things and when many have the ego of a small country, this leads them to venture into businesses and areas where they know little or nothing about. With that comes an assortment of problems. Just because you were a good player, does not make you an expert on many things in the business world. All you really know is how to play a recreational game better than most. How many are prepared to retrain and get the proper advice on how to take the long steps up that are required in order for them to start getting and then being able to keep a so called proper job that the family can rely on.

Many look to get into sectors that they still consider to have a coolness associated to them like owning a bar or getting into property. It's nearly always property as that can mean so many things to so many different people. It's also a business that will run nicely alongside picking up some well needed cash for playing club cricket or playing for Lashings or Old England if you've been lucky enough to reach those heights. The goal is to have the same success and lifestyle as before the axe fell on their sporting career and the curtains came down, but a goal without a decent plan in place to back it up is I'm afraid nothing more than a wish.

It was at a Lashings match that I'd been invited to attend a few years ago that I had the misfortune to be sat on a table with an ex England international who had only recently retired. It appeared he was there almost out of duress in order to pick up his £400 appearance fee for rolling his arm over and hitting a few boundaries. Still decent money if you've been good enough to have played at that level. However, over lunch when asked as to his future business plans, he looked down at the rest of the table as if how dare they have the temerity to ask such a question to someone like him. The answer was a fairly bland one in that he was going into property development and that was about it. When I asked him if this was something he'd been doing in the off season, or as a side line whilst still playing, he started sarcastically asking if I knew what I was talking about and that he knew lots about the property game. He'd worked with some companies he'd met through his benefit year after all. Hardly MBA stuff if we're honest, but he'd played international sport so that trumps most things when it comes to arguments with ex pros. If you're discussing cricket, playing the test card can normally win you most rows, but when it comes to other subjects, telling someone you've played for England doesn't somehow always seem the most appropriate answer when the business plan looks like its been completed by a teenager.

This I replied was the huge mistake I made about the business I went into when all I really knew about in reality was cricket and coaching sport. I knew nothing about accounting principles or stock taking, pricing or sales techniques and it cost me and my family a small fortune to put right over the next few years once I decided to turn the lights off and move onto something else.

Anyway, he not surprisingly decided against the advice of myself and a couple of the other well meaning folk on the table and it was with interest when I read that three years later this player had gone bankrupt owing millions after a failed development project had gone badly wrong. It appeared from the press coverage that he had taken some very poor decisions when it came who he chose to go into business with added to a stunning lack of knowledge relating to a complex industry. The worse aspect was that he had persuaded several of his friends and ex team mates to invest and all had to take the financial hit with him. Tragically, some lost their life savings. No matter who you are, the chances of you getting that kind of money back again is next to none.

It seems sad that many sportsmen and women seem to have the ability to attract the wrong kind of partners and it is a worrying statistic that many ex players are as good as bankrupt as early as two years after retiring from the sporting arena. Many are prone to some sort of poor man's hustler's paradise who think that the pitfalls and problems are never going to happen to them. With the fact that they haven't earnt anywhere near the money that footballers and even less like the cash earnt by the major American sports will have made at the same period of time, it comes down more to the loss of status and of having a purpose in your life. It might not be that sexy to work in an office or in insurance, but you might not get into financial trouble all the same. Unless you are in the top one percent of ex players with book deals and TV offers waiting at your table, you are going to have to get what you've never had before and that's a regular job.

Ramblings No. 4
ALL THOSE EGOS IN ONE DRESSING ROOM

There is a fairly common belief among ex-sportspeople that, once they stop playing at any level, the thing they miss most is the dressing room. The dressing room is the inner sanctum of any sport, the place where bat throwing and major hissy fits are mixed in with deafening silences as well as being the theatre for the characters to perform their weekly traditions and hold court while others sit and listen. People miss the banter and the chance to laugh and talk utter nonsense, where you can relax and be yourself away from the pressures of home and family as well as the time to reflect on successes and failures with your mates. To sit and just enjoy being part of a team. Of all the things I miss about playing, it's the dressing room I miss the most.

However, for all the times when it was great to put your feet up after a win or a superb performance, there was also the side of the dressing room that not many get to see. The rows, the fights, the disagreements and the personal issues all had a part to play in what made up most changing rooms. For all the good things that went on, there were equally as many where the personality clashes made for just as much interest. But, despite all these points, nothing comes close to the main source of so many problems that can affect a team and all the characters who share that dressing room: Ego.

Is ego a good thing or a bad thing? Is it always the loudest players who automatically have the biggest egos? And at what point does it start to drive that person away from what has made them successful in the first place? When you have so many different egos and personalities within four walls it is fascinating to hang around long enough to see what happens. From where I stand, it's the subject that, in all my years in the game, interests me the most.

I will be the first to admit there are certain parts of my make up where having the ego the size of a planet has helped me overcome certain challenges when others weren't able to. There is a thin line between confidence and arrogance and it's this line that is sometimes the hardest to navigate. Let me explain. Rightly or wrongly, I believed that, when it came to bowling a cricket ball, I thought I was good enough to get anyone on the planet out on any given day of the week and I mean anybody. Be it Mark or Steve Waugh or Mark Smith or Steve Jones, I didn't much care. I believed that, if I performed at my best, I could bowl a delivery that would have been wasted on a club player but would have been nicked by a top level player. They would be on their way back to the pavilion and my point would be proved. I also firmly believed that if you were going to commit to playing this game at a decent level, then you had to believe you had enough quality to do the job, otherwise what the hell were you doing out on the pitch in the first place?

271

I backed my ability and thankfully the scorebooks show that, on many occasions, it worked as I had the knack of claiming the opposition's prize scalp many times. There were obviously times when it didn't go to plan but you must always back yourself to succeed. Sometimes that sheer bloody mindedness was what got the job done when many around you fell by the wayside.

When you list the characteristics of what makes a big ego I seem to have rather a lot of them, and in spades. It must be in the genes. Confidence, yes; could be self-centred, mmmm yes; always has an opinion, most definitely; could be difficult to handle, err, possibly; and the list goes on. It doesn't make you feel too good about yourself when you read them, but the two sides of the ego debate need to work together in order for that person to perform. Are they confident because they know they have the ability to perform or are they just bigheaded arrogant bastards? Possibly both. However, it's a certainty that the higher up the ladder you go in terms of professional sport or business or in the arts, the egos you meet are king sized by comparison with the ones you have come across before because they almost certainly needed that sense of belief and inner confidence to rise to that level in the first place. If you don't believe in yourself, then who will? If you think you have a gift, surely it's your job to unlock that potential and make the best out of yourself because, like it or not, your talent is only ever on loan and you can be 100 per cent sure that, one day, age will catch up with you and that loan will be called in

As this topic of ego seems to be one of those yin and yang type subjects, it's only fair to ask that, on the other side of the coin, did people who achieved less than they had hoped not try hard enough? Did they do all in their power to change the situation for the better? Did they work hard and dedicate themselves like some others? The answer is almost certainly not, so the easiest thing to do is to blame somebody else.

Where this gets out of hand is when you take those egotistical beliefs away from your subject of expertise and into your daily life. It's well known that, just because you have been a high achiever in one sphere of business or sport, it does not mean you are an expert on every subject on the planet. Once, at the pre-season party of a former international cricketer, the person in charge of cooking the meat got so sick of all the advice coming his way from his celebrated host he said that, "although the host might have scored way more first class runs, it didn't make him an expert on how to do a f*****g barbeque" before getting into his car and storming off.

From the village green team through to good club sides and up to county and Test levels, you will still find the same characters sitting in the same seats every week. The size and splendour of the changing rooms might be very different but I can guarantee you that the people who dwell in them will be very similar. Some people are natural loners, some are piss takers who seem to find a target at every opportunity, and some are mavericks who tend to be wild and hard to predict but, in a team environment, always necessary. Love them or hate them – and that in possible in equal measure – you know you need them and you can bet your bottom dollar they know you need them. Add to that the players who are always trying to take the team forward and setting new goals who, not surprisingly, tend to clash with the ones who favour a more conservative approach. There will also be the two rutting stags that seem to have a simmering feud but because they have a slight fear of each other and what might end up being said in public, they both choose to stay clear of each other week after week, season after season.

There is nowhere on earth where there is more straight talking than a dressing room. In there, everything comes out, often in spades, to the extent that it is some player's worst nightmare to be called out in the one place they treat as their version of church. Will the no-nonsense talking toughen them up and make them better prepared for the struggles to come? Or will it send them running out of the club claiming they are misunderstood and not shown enough love? Some will appreciate it, take it on board and come back better for the experience, while others won't ever accept it, never forget it and hate you for being so brutal. With the introduction of the huge statistical based packages that now come with all modern sport, the likes of cricket and golf can give you the facts that, after time, will make the arguments null and void. Have you scored enough runs to play at this level and above? Do you take enough top order wickets to move to the next level? If the answer is obvious, you need to be honest enough to admit the fact that, season after season, the book simply doesn't lie.

At all levels, there have been myths about certain players but these stats packages have put those to bed. Even if you have talent and someone in authority thinks you have a chance of progressing to the next level, the simple fact is that, if you are not succeeding at the level below, you have very little chance of progressing much further. If you are only averaging 30 or not bowling club sides out, how will you do against full time professionals on the county circuit? You might not want to believe what the wise heads in your own dressing room are telling you but you can rest assured that someone in the next dressing room up will – and it might not be what you want to hear.

Like it or not, the dressing room you are in is probably the right one. If you were much better, you'd be in a different one, higher up the pecking order with its different conversations, opinions and characters. If you've had the pleasure of being in such places, you're not there now because you are either too old or you've been sacked. That can understandably cause some bitterness but it's the place in which you currently operate and, unless you're young enough to have the aspiration and the ability to go higher, then it's the place you're going to stay until you decide you've either had enough or you're prepared to slide down the levels just to keep playing.

The thing for me now is that I don't miss the travelling, I don't miss the chance to play on the best grounds around, I don't miss aching all week just to get ready to do it all again and I don't really miss performing well against the best players out there. I've done all that, many times over. What I do miss more than anything though is sitting with my mates in the dressing room and putting the world to rights. That is what I miss the most and, I guess, I always will.

Ramblings No. 5

IT'LL BE A DIFFERENT GAME IN TEN YEARS

Ben is ten years old and an extremely nice young man. Well-mannered and polite, funny and, it has to be said for someone so young, pretty good at sport. He is enthusiastic, attentive and eminently coachable, a bit of a rarity these days. Today is the first match of the season and Ben was so excited last night he could not sleep. But when morning comes, so does the bad weather. The sky is turning darker by the minute and it begins to rain. The weather gets worse, the match is called off before the stumps even get into the ground and, for Ben, the excitement has turned to disaster and nothing is going to cheer him up for hours. For most of his team it's not the end of the world, and for some it's a relief, but to see Ben's face in the changing rooms takes you back to what what you were like at his age, when playing was simply the be all and end all of your life and reminds you why you fell in love with this stupid game in the first place.

For Ben, he has years ahead of him while I have just finished playing and, out of the two of us, I suppose he is the lucky one. He has his youth and some talent while I'm an old fossil who creeks way too much and should have given up years ago. The thing that worries me though is what will happen if Ben and his mates want to play league cricket in a few years' time? It's a subject that is starting to worry a lot of other people too because, for many, the dark clouds have started to roll in.

In 2014 the ECB reported that almost 65,000 fewer people were actually playing than at the time of the previous survey. Now statistics can often be read any way you wish but the one that frightens me the most is that, during the same period, more than 5% of matches were forfeited and, even more alarmingly, another 5% of all matches were played without the full 11 players. So why is this happening and what's causing the players to walk away?

IT ALL STARTS WITH THE SCHOOLS

In the battle of the schoolyard, cricket is still struggling to compete with other sports and, I guess, with the pace of life in general. Despite the excellent work of the Chance to Shine programme, the amount of cricket now played in state schools is at an alarmingly low level. For many head teachers, cricket takes up a long period of time and has a high capital outlay in terms of coaches, facilities and equipment. Unless you have a head of department who loves cricket, then the coaching will be left to the PE teacher who plays football or rugby or to the PE co-ordinator who just wants to make sure that nobody gets hurt in their lesson. Add this to the frustrations of previous overspending which has led to many schools being over budget before the term starts and the problems are clear. How to fix them is another matter and, unless you have a magic wand or a ton of money, these problems may be terminal.

TOO MUCH BLOODY FOOTBALL

Almost four times as many children play football than any other sport. It is the national pastime and dominates sports coverage in the media. No matter how much other sports might succeed, even at world level, they all pale into insignificance when compared with the attention football generates throughout the year. The most obvious advantage football has over other sports is that it's simple and cheap to play. Some kids, a pair of trainers, some jumpers for goalposts and a ball and you're away. Now I love my football and have played and followed it all my life but clubs and schools spend a frightening amount of time on it, to the detriment of other good sports. Long gone are the days when people played football in the winter and then a summer sport like cricket. Now, with the competition for places at clubs getting so intense, children and parents feel they can't miss out on the various tournaments that go on during the summer, meaning there is little point trying your hand at another sport. Add that to the number of parents with delusions that their child is destined for the Premier League and it's even harder to get talented youngsters to play cricket.

IT TAKES TOO LONG THESE DAYS

We now live in a world where information and data is available at the touch of a button and everything about our lives is set up to be quicker and more reliable. For young children today, the thought of travelling to a match, spending 40 overs in the field with no mobile and then spending another 40 overs waiting for your side to bat is just not what they want to do with their lives. It's simply too long. "A 20-over match is long enough, Sir," they used to tell me.

TOO INTERESTED IN SOCIAL MEDIA

In some families, asking children – and, in many cases, parents – to put their phones away long enough to sit down and have a meal together is often enough cause for argument so to get a teen-ager to be without their mobile for around an hour while they field is like asking them to stick pins in their legs while they go all Kevin and Perry at you. At one school, I did a phone check as the players left the changing room as the delightful youths tried to find different ways of hiding their devices. You've got little or no chance of getting a youngster to score, I'm afraid, even if there is an app for it. In my youth, there was always someone who loved to watch and came along just to score but you don't find them about anymore.

LACK OF CONCENTRATION AND PATIENCE

Without wishing to sound like an old git and annoying my children in the process, the rise in mobile phones, social media and the faster pace of life has meant that the concentration levels of young children is now worryingly low. It's a problem that all teachers and coaches will testify to, so for a sport like cricket, where concentration is such a huge part of the skills of the game as well as the need for some occasional patience, then it really becomes a worry. With other team sports like football, rugby or hockey, your child can be involved in the game at any time, but the nature of cricket doesn't allow for that and so, at times, the lack of patience when the children aren't batting or bowling is frightening. It's become that classic Catch 22 problem where, if you don't give them all a game all of the time, then there is a fair chance they won't come back for more.

BETTER START POOLING RESOURCES

Many clubs are now struggling to get the same number of players out at the weekend as they did in previous seasons. Three teams become two for a season before the seconds are starting to have the same selection issues as the third team used to have and so on.

The fall in membership also adds to the financial pressures at a club which, instead of aiming to do well in whatever league they are in, just concentrate on getting enough players out to fulfil the fixtures and to hell with the outcome. It's all about survival until we get some new blood. For many, it's the classic death by a thousand cuts where one problem follows another until the time comes for everyone to stop hurting and call it a day. Clubs are either folding or merging with a stronger local side, meaning that everyone can at least get a game and, for the time being at least, carry on playing.

FAMILY TIME

When I started playing you were part of a giant family where players, wives and young children travelled round the circuit together watching countless hours hoping their chosen man had a good day while chatting over tea and drinks and then probably ending up in a pub somewhere on the way home. All very Darling Buds of May it seemed with my rose-tinted spectacles on. Like them or loathe them, those days are well and truly gone as modern life has taken over, meaning that wives often work full time and don't want to watch cricket on precious days off, children now have lots more things on offer to entertain them and most families are just not prepared to give up that amount of time anymore.

IS TV TO BLAME?

When the Sky TV deal was signed long ago, it was generally seen as a great day for the ECB and the counties and not such a good one for the armchair fan. With no live cricket on terrestrial television the public have been starved of watching the national summer game unless you pay at least £50 a month to have Gower, Botham and Lloyd tell you that England have gone out of the

World Cup at the group stages yet again. There is no doubt that the Sky millions have made the average county cricketer much wealthier and that a lot of the money has funded numerous development projects all over country but, for better or worse, the ECB is now stuck with Sky. There is no turning back because the finances are now so great. What this means, though, is that the next generation will miss out on watching the best players in action live on TV and so won't be running out into the garden to have a go, just like I and millions of others like me did all those years ago. Having said that, it is certainly the case that the TV watching habits of today are very different and, if my children and their friends are anything to go by, they rarely sit down to watch live broadcasts anyway and prefer to watch programmes on catch up on their laptops. Hopefully the recently announced deal from the ECB that some live cricket will be returning to the BBC screens in 2020 will make a telling difference.

COACHING PROBLEMS

In an attempt to get as many coaches as possible, we have failed to see the alarming holes in the standard of coaching that goes on in our clubs and schools. With the new UK coaching badges covering a wider range of topics and focusing less on the actual skills and technical side of the game, many children are being given a raw deal in terms of what they are being taught. Participation is hugely important but we need to make sure children are given every opportunity to succeed. I recognise this is the classic chicken and egg situation, that without volunteers to coach in the first place, there would be no junior sections. However, much of the coaching I have witnessed recently has been of such a poor standard that the children are not being given the technical help to allow them to survive and then excel enough for them to want to come back for another go. If you're regularly getting cleaned up in the first few balls or being sent into orbit every time you bowl then it won't take long for you to decide that cricket might not be the game for you. Simply, if they don't get good enough to enjoy their experiences they will become disillusioned and go off and find another sport to play.

CLUB PROBLEMS

Lack of players, rising costs, failing to deal with the fall in subscriptions, children and young people not coming through the doors as much, too much paperwork, Clubmark problems, paying too much for Sky TV, way too much aggravation with CRBs and DBS's. The list goes on and on.

Clubs have always faced problems but it seems that there are now more than in years gone by. Many larger clubs aiming for county and national honours look to attract a wealthy benefactor to help pay the bills but this can lead to other problems further down the line. The benefactor can quickly become a dictator if he falls out with the senior management and then, before you know it, that kind offer of an annual cheque is a distant memory. For most smaller clubs, it's the problems of falling numbers and commitment and the rising cost of equipment and facilities that keep chairmen up at night. That, and the fairly important matter of making sure all the teams have 11 players for the weekend.

WHERE WILL WE BE IN 20 YEARS' TIME?

If you have read this far, you will know I have some fears for the future of the game I love but it's not all doom and gloom. I've tried to be honest while still being hopeful that cricket will start to flourish again soon. Many clubs in different parts of the country will tell a story of high numbers and endless children playing in competitive leagues with no financial worries in the slightest and I wish them the best and hope they continue to prosper.

What I do think will happen in the next ten to 20 years is that the recreational game will morph into a shorter timeframe, similar to the time spent playing football or rugby, and the all-day games against the best teams in the county that I so enjoyed will become a thing of the past. There will just not be enough interest to sustain such a long day away from home. The time spent on the motorways and A roads will be less as leagues become more centralised and talented players, those who shine at the 20-over level, will be picked out by the counties, David Warner-style, who in turn will hope they have the ability to learn to play the longer formats of the game that the first class teams will demand.

With Twenty20 leagues becoming more popular by the year, I and people my age will be replaced by a different set of cricketers who, I guess, will look for different pleasures from the ones we enjoyed during our peak years. To them, I hope they enjoy it as much as I did and pass the game on to the next generation who will, in turn, do the same. That is the point of it all, isn't it?

Ramblings No. 6

EDUCATION

One of the most bizarre things about what I've ended up doing for most of my working life is that a huge chunk of it has been spent in various educational establishments. To be honest I'm still not sure how that happened to me as I don't look back on my school days with much fondness and was only too delighted to leave when I had the chance.

For all that, I am eternally grateful that I have been given the chance to work with so many brilliant and entertaining children all over the world, who gave me the chance to get paid for throwing or kicking a ball around whilst telling jokes of a fairly poor standard. Some have grown up and become friends and I have also been lucky to spend my time with many sensational teachers and coaches who make the day worthwhile just by spending time with them. I am one of those rare people in this world who is lucky enough not to worry what day of the week it is, because, for the majority of my life, I've looked forward to going to work.

Not that it's been all sunshine and roses, there have been one or two little darlings, the odd set of unhinged parents as well as a couple of head teachers and heads of department who I seem to forget when it comes to the Christmas card list. However, no job ever comes without its problems and, for someone who has been doing it since 1991 and as I move towards the end of my coaching career, I would say that I'm still well ahead on points and delighted it has gone the way it has.

From where I sit, the children and their reactions, improvements and achievements are the best part of what is arguably the most rewarding job around. Having had the chance to work in both the state and independent sectors, I suppose I've been able to assess where the world of coaching and education has moved onto from both the teachers' and the parents' point of view and how it has changed in the 26 years I've been involved. So, after all that time, you do wonder what you would tell your younger self if they were about to enter the world of education today. As I see it, plenty has changed since 1991 and there are now far more pitfalls awaiting youngsters today than ever before.

CHANGING RELATIONSHIPS

One major change over the last 30 or so years is the relationship between parents and children to the extent that, today, parents pander to their children far more than in previous generations and many seem afraid to upset them in any shape or form if it means them not getting what they want. The days of children amusing themselves during the school holidays seem to have long gone and the children of today wait expectantly to find out what exciting things their parents have planned for them. The idea of getting on your bike and turning left to the football pitches or turning right to the cricket ground before getting back in time for tea are a thing of the past. All very nice in the main but the real question is: Has it created a generation with such huge entitlement and very little imagination or willingness to do anything for themselves?

DEALING WITH UNREALISTIC EXPECTATIONS

This has risen hugely over the years. We all love our children and try to do all we can to make sure they are successful and happy. What appears to have changed most is the unrealistic expectations children have for themselves and that parents put on their children and teachers, schools or clubs. For many, just because you show some early talent or love for a subject, an instrument or a sport does not make you destined for Hollywood. It simply doesn't. It is the same reality when it comes to your child's grades, getting into their next school or trying to get selected to go on a professional sports club's youth set up. The moment you mention anything positive then the parents take it as a guarantee of success and they will hold that against you if it doesn't happen. Everyone is different, everyone matures at different stages and so trying to make predictions is almost impossible. When it comes to sport, the chances of making it to a professional are close to nil. Many have high hopes that the improbable might happen but, despite all the quality coaching and hours you might put in, reality strikes and it is often the coach who gets the blame for those wasted teenage years. If you're honest enough to tell it like you see it, parents can accuse you of shattering their children's dreams. Sometimes you just can't win.

EVERYTHING'S SUGAR COATED

Sometimes things in life don't go according to plan. You don't end up playing for Real Madrid, or on stage in the West End, having a number one record or marrying the Victoria's Secret model. That's just life, I'm afraid. Sometimes it can be cruel and it has happened to all of us at some stage and will continue to do so until our final days. For in today's world, where everybody gets a medal no matter where you finish, there is a fine line between rewarding success on one hand and giving people the excuses they need when they have not applied themselves, as they should have. We seem to have lost the right to fail at anything these days to the extent that getting a C is classed as the end of the world as we know it. So mediocre is no longer allowed and yet the problem is, when all around are getting high grades just to please children and parents alike, we seem to have forgotten what excellence really looks like. As we often learn more about ourselves when we lose or things don't go so well, are we actually allowing the children to learn some valuable life skills before they come back and try again? This is often the subject that causes the most disagreements between staff members, the line between allowing children to gain the confidence to progress and having the actual grasp of a subject to allow that to happen.

WAY TOO MUCH DOCUMENTATION

With today's ways of reporting systems and identifying talent or problems, this has created a mountain of documents and paperwork that have to be filled in before anything practical can start. If even a proportion of that time could be spent on coaching or teaching, then surely the children would benefit. With profiling systems now starting at three years of age we are now looking at any method of making sure that square pegs really do go into square holes. Attend any parents' evening and you may well be greeted by a huge stack of data that shows how your child is coming along, or not, as the case may be. Add to that the fact that we've been testing kids to death and it only makes for more form filling but strangely there never seems to be a box to tick for the children who will develop at different stages in their lives. Ending up just assessing children rather than teaching them can now become the norm, when surely it should be the other way around. The age-old argument regarding long holidays pales into insignificance when the amount of documentation is taken into account and its effect on moral and the ability to do your primary role properly.

SOCIAL MEDIA AND ITS PROBLEMS

Oh where to begin on this one? With the arrival of emails and social media, the ability to communicate between children, parents and the school or club has its undoubted advantages and, on the whole, everyone uses the system for what it was intended. But, as in all areas of life, the use of emails and the like has allowed people to vent their frustrations publicly when it probably would have been better not to have pressed the send button. The culture of emailing over every single aspect of their children's activities has created a mountain of extra work when that time would have better served on the pupils themselves. The amount of emails sent after eight or nine o'clock when the chardonnay has kicked in and people want to get something off their chest is really quite worrying. It's not called the "wine o'clock email" for nothing. For all that, the real problem is that frustration then gets passed on to the WhatsApp chatroom and, before you know it, people with no idea of the facts have created a problem the teacher or coach knows nothing about. However, the real winner here is the Mumsnet generation and its keyboard warriors who sit behind a codename around midnight and start commenting on schools, clubs and teachers without realising the damage they are doing to people's reputations and future prospects. All because someone might have told you their honest opinions about your child. If you feel the need to write about your nightmare experience in Pizza Express or the fact that your child's emotional development is being hampered because your builder hasn't finished your extension, then that's your business. Sadly, in many cases it's utterly poisonous and I'm afraid to say it happens far more than most people realise.

LACK OF MONEY

Let's not kid ourselves here; you're not going to be paid a fortune if you go into coaching or teaching. You can earn a nice salary with the benefits that go with it but you're not going to end up as the CEO of a multi-national. The older children and their parents will have some idea of what you, as a teacher, will earn and some can make rude comments about that, especially if you have a disagreement over their child. You hope the people who enter the profession do so not because they think it's an easy option with long holidays and the chance of a free ski-ing trip now and then but because it's something they really want to do. A professional calling, some say, and that's the way it should be.

WHERE HAVE THE MAVERICKS GONE?

In a sanitised world of political correctness, social media and too much parent power, the role of the talented maverick is slowly eroding from the system and, for my money, that's a terribly sad thing. The person who goes out of their way to make sure the children have a brilliant time and makes the lessons or coaching sessions fun and entertaining, are the ones that you remember when you leave school, not the ones who didn't have the imagination to make their subject more enjoyable. Now, more so than ever before, there are so many potential land mines in the world of education that some teachers, no matter how talented they are, take the easy option and do just enough so they get no comeback from parents or head teachers. Despite being desperate to do more, they feel the handcuffs are on so tightly they aren't prepared to go that extra mile

TOO MUCH PARENT POWER

I think my parents went up to my school to complain about something maybe once or twice in all the years I went there. It was under the promise that I really was telling the truth and they wouldn't be told something that they might not want to hear. Nowadays, parents are such regular visitors to the head teacher's office, wanting to discuss something that might not have much to do with the running of the school and all based on what their child has told them. They never go to the teacher or the coach who has their child, they go straight to the head and that's where the problems start. For, no matter where we are in life and whatever we do, nearly every story has two sides and, despite it being told so convincingly in an email or sitting in the head's office, I can guarantee that nine times out of ten it probably didn't always happen like that. What you would love would be for a head teacher to ask their staff to be allowed to do their job and for the parents to trust their judgment and, on many occasions, to stop wasting their time, as there are far more important things to be doing. The value of a strong head that backs their staff cannot be understated but they are becoming fewer by the years, I'm afraid.

EVERYONE'S AN EXPERT

I don't tell you how to run your company. I don't tell you how to be a civil engineer. I don't tell you how to sell stocks and shares or advertising. I don't tell you how to be a surgeon or a nurse. You get the picture, I'm sure. But, because everyone has spent an element of their youth in the classroom or the sports fields, then that makes them an expert when it comes to education and what makes up the qualities of being a good teacher or a good coach. They have never sat in your classroom or taken part in one of your coaching sessions but quite freely comment on what they think are your strengths and weaknesses without having a clue about the facts. The days when people took your word are, sadly, fading fast. For good teaching and coaching is a highly under-valued art form but too many people think it's nothing more than money for old jam.

WHERE HAVE THE MANNERS GONE?

The thorny subject of how children behave and what is acceptable is one that has rumbled on not only in schools and clubs but also between families and friends for as long as anyone can remember. For the children themselves it can be hard, because you can bet your bottom dollar that, at any school or club you go, there will be a huge differential between what some teachers allow and what some will crack down on immediately. Is someone being too strict or is someone being walked all over? The most frightening thing is if you have to tell a child's parents that their behaviour is a problem then, normally, all hell breaks loose. You can often tell the children who behave beautifully and the ones who don't by how some speak to their parents or, worse still, how some of the parents speak to people. Sometimes you do wonder whether the kids had any chance to begin with. You can't leave your manners outside if you haven't actually been taught any. A lot of teachers and coaches now feel completely handcuffed when it comes to disciplining children for they have no real powers to do anything and I'm afraid that many children, certainly in secondary education, know that all too well. The answer is that many will just simply take the easy option and let it slide.

IS IT TEACHING CHILDREN ABOUT REAL LIFE?

My observations are based on the changes I have seen over the years and how it affects the many brilliant people who have chosen to go into what is still a very challenging profession. It's not all doom and gloom and I've been incredibly fortunate to have been involved in it for many years. The real question for me is whether we are preparing children for life after school well enough. Have we prepared them for a future where the most important aspects are their work ethic and the ability to form good working relationship with other people? We need to allow children to develop at their own pace and not tutor them to death just to get them to the next level of education and to hell with the consequences. It's an impossible question to answer and one where you will get 100 different answers from 100 different people. For everyone's idea of what good looks like is different and that in turn makes it impossible to please all the people all of the time. Still, what do I know?